Scripture quotations, unless otherwise indicated, are taken from *The Holy Bible, New International Version*®, *NIV*® Copyright © 1973, 1978, 1984, 2011 by Biblica, Inc.™ Used by permission. All rights reserved worldwide.

Scripture quotations from the *Holy Bible*, New Living Translation, copyright ©1996, 2004, 2007 by Tyndale House Foundation. Used by permission of Tyndale House Publishers, Inc., Carol Stream, Illinois 60188. All rights reserved.

Scripture quotations from THE MESSAGE. Copyright © by Eugene H. Peterson 1993, 1994, 1995, 1996, 2000, 2001, 2002. Used by permission of Tyndale House Publishers, Inc. All rights reserved.

Photo credit (c) smarnad www.fotosearch.com

Printed in the United States of America
First Printing, 2014
ISBN 13:978-0692223970

ACKNOWLEDGEMENTS

The ideas in this book express how Jesus Christ has formed and shaped himself in me for three decades. To my Lord, and those he has used in my formation - thank you for influencing the writing of this book. To my birth parents and parents by marriage - thank you for the nurture and solid foundation you gave me in Christ. To my mentors in Christ and ministry: Dr. Gordon Zimmerman, William Thomas Saxon, Dr. James R. Tozer, Don Roth and Dr. Jay Kesler - thank you for all you poured into me. To the hospitable staff of Miracle Camp - thanks for a place to write; and to the leadership team of Crossroads Evangelical Church - thanks for the time to write. To the people of Crossroads Evangelical Church - thanks for sharing life in Christ with me and the experiences of pouring out our souls to the Savior through joyous, challenging and traumatic times. Thanks to Barb Weis, Sherrill Woodard, Darla Rupp, Kerry Morris, Levi Stuckey, Mary Mueller and Jared Oyer whose editorial perspectives, work and patience contributed much to this work. Thanks to my wife Lanita, children Luke and Lindsey, Nick and Megan, Mark and Audrey and Kevin, whose steady presence and encouragement kept me writing when I wanted to quit. And finally, thank you, Lord Jesus, for relentlessly compelling and pressing me to express in writing some of the ways you have formed yourself in me.

TABLE OF CONTENTS

Introduction
How Hungry Are You?

"I'm so hungry!" Mary, a dear elderly woman, spoke these words over and over in the last years of her life as she wandered the halls of the nursing home looking for something to eat. It didn't matter if she had just eaten lunch or had a snack in her hand while she said it, the crippling effect of old age dementia had stolen her sense of reality, causing her to think she was always hungry. No matter how many snacks the nursing personnel gave Mary between meals, or how much she consumed at breakfast, lunch and supper, the halls of the convalescent center continually rang with her desperate cry, "I'm so hungry!" Mary's compulsive desire to eat and her abnormal craving for food seemed insatiable. "I'm so hungry" ought to be the insatiable cry of every believer's heart.

Jesus interacted with people who seemed to be insatiably hungry like Mary. The day after Jesus miraculously fed five thousand, they chased him around the lake in search of more food. Jesus challenged the hungry crowd to pursue a different kind of food. "Do not work for food that spoils, but for food that endures to eternal life..." (*New International Version*, John 6:27a). When the crowd asked what work they needed to do, Jesus said, "The work of God is this: to believe in the one he has sent." (John 6:29). In the discourse that followed, Jesus repeated this synonym for "work," "believe," several times in association with eternal life (John 6:40, 47). Jesus associated two other words with eternal life in this passage: "eat" and "feed." "If anyone eats of this bread he will live forever. . . Whoever eats my flesh and drinks my blood has eternal life. . . So the one who feeds on me will live because of me. . . He who feeds on this bread will live forever." (John 6:51b, 54a, 57b, 58b).

Four themes from Jesus' instruction in John 6 shape the need and practice of spiritual consumption:
1. Centrality of Christ in biblical revelation (v 35)
2. Necessity of Christ's life formed in the human heart (v 56)
3. Feeding is believing (vs 47, 54)
4. Personal responsibility to feed on Jesus (v 53)

These themes, properly understood and applied, form the theological foundation of *Consuming Christ*. Practically, I want to help people understand that to believe in Jesus is to feed on Jesus. My prayer is that readers will not only understand but begin feeding on Jesus.

A side by side comparison of the verbs and objects of these texts reveals that the verbs ("believe," eats," "drinks" and "feeds") must be synonymous since the object of each verb is the same: eternal or everlasting life.

> 6:40 "everyone who looks to the son and believes in him shall have eternal life"
> 6:54 "eats my flesh and drinks my blood has eternal life"
> 6:47 "he who believes has everlasting life"
> 6:51 "if anyone eats of this bread he will live forever"
> 6:57 "the one who feeds on me will live because of me"
> 6:58 "he who feeds on this bread will live forever."

If "believe" and the verbs used for feeding are not synonymous, then there must be more than one way of eternal life, and that is not consistent with the rest of the New Testament.

Jesus used forms of the words "believe," "eat" and "feed" synonymously and interchangeably in this text, but with a consistent object—eternal life. Jesus taught that eternal life is appropriated by believing or "feeding" on him: **feeding is believing**. This feeding on or believing in Jesus is the "work" (John 6:29) God has for us in response to the gospel. In John 6:53 Jesus said it in the negative, "I tell you the truth, unless you eat the flesh of the Son of Man and drink his blood, you have no life in you."

So why do we think so infrequently about this life-changing metaphor of what believing in Jesus really means? Some interpret John 6:53-58 only as a symbolic reference to sharing the Lord 's Supper or Eucharist but fail to apprehend the depth of Jesus' instruction about belief. The metaphor, feeding is believing, is more involved than a simple point of comparison to accepting Jesus. The people in the crowd that day understood there was a greater depth to Jesus' instruction, and that's what made his teaching so hard to digest (John 6:60). Many turned back and no longer followed him (John 6:66). When Jesus asked the twelve if they wanted to leave, Peter said, 'To whom shall we go? You have the words of eternal life" (John 6:68). Eternal life is found in Jesus alone. To feed on Jesus is to live, because feeding is believing.

If faith does not include an actual receiving of the life of Jesus through feeding on him, then the life of Christ will not form within the human soul; and Christ formed within the believer is the essence of the gospel, "Christ in you, the hope of glory" (Col. 1:27b). We need to think more seriously about this instructional metaphor of feeding on Jesus. Metaphors, when pondered, impart deeper understanding of the subject; and this subject is primary—eternal life. The word "life" is used thirteen times in John 6, each time in reference to Jesus himself as food that gives life. Few passages in scripture teach assurance of life from God more emphatically than John 6. Yet even a cursory reading of the chapter reveals that life is appropriated through feeding on Jesus. Jesus said feeding on him would result in a glorious union: "Whoever eats my flesh and drinks my blood remains in me and I in him" (John 6:56). Jesus forms his life in the believer who feeds on him.

Paul worked tirelessly that Christ might be formed in the Galatians, "My dear children, for whom I am again in the pains of childbirth until Christ is formed in you" (Gal. 4:19). John affirmed the necessity of this internal formation of the life of Christ in his first letter, "He who has the Son has life; he who does not have the Son of God does not have life" (1 John 5:12). The word translated "have" in this verse carries the sense of "containing or being possessed with" rather than just holding on to something. Any person whose soul does not contain the Son does not have life. The formation of the life of Christ in the human soul is the hope of glory. The cliché *"You are what you eat"* rings true spiritually. Only food that is consumed and digested imparts life.

But saving faith is often taught as mere intellectual assent to the facts of the gospel, which ignores the necessity of the life of Christ being formed in the believer. Jesus was broken and poured out on the cross so that he might be formed within believers, not just so believers would know what he did. Romans 10:9 declares, "If you confess with your mouth, 'Jesus is Lord' and believe in your heart that God raised him from the dead, you will be saved." "Belief" is not synonymous with "confess" in this text; they are different ideas. Confession is a declaration of the mouth. Belief is an ongoing response of the heart, earlier described as feeding. Feeding on Jesus is unnecessary if the idea of believing is reduced to declaring the facts of the gospel. But believing is feeding, as Jesus clearly taught, and without feeding there is no life. "Unless you eat the flesh of the Son of Man and drink his blood, you have no life in you" (John 6:53).

The idea that salvation can be gained through intellectual agreement with the facts of the gospel alone (a human decision) leads to two non-gospel poles of behavior: gross immorality and moralism. The fruit of immorality is inconsistent with gospel fruit, while moralism leads to a human-manufactured or plastic "fruit." For such persons, the life of Christ is more an example to be emulated by human effort than the actual presence of Christ forming in the soul of the believer. Moralistic thinking embraces Jesus' ethical standard of behavior but has no need for the life of Christ to be anything but exemplary. Moralistic people try harder when they fail but fail to feed on Jesus. Instead of pouring out failure to the Savior and asking for the life of Christ to fill him and change him, the moralist simply tries harder. His repentance is expressed by, "I will work harder to be more like Christ" instead of repentance which says, "I will feed more on Jesus so the life of Christ will form in and change me by the power of the Spirit."

My hope in writing this book is to stir the reader to seriously contemplate what Jesus meant by saying, "The one who feeds on me will live because of me" (John 6:57). This is the primary metaphor of the book, but many other related metaphors are used. Think deeply and prayerfully about Jesus' metaphor and the others in this book. God will give you rich insight and experience of feeding on Jesus as you meditate on Jesus' instruction in John 6.

Love for malnourished believers compelled me to write this book. Those who feed on Jesus now will be chosen to feed with Jesus at a future heavenly banquet. Jesus said a relative few will be chosen for this banquet and outside the banquet room there will be weeping and gnashing of teeth (Luke 13:24-30). Those who thought they'd be first in may be last or won't get in at all.

The way in is narrow and only a few find it. An ongoing response of faith to God's initiative of grace is the way into the banquet. I've become convinced that such faith means feeding on Jesus—believing is feeding.

After laying more of a theological foundation in the first two chapters, we'll consider how to practically feed on Jesus based on examples from scripture and illustrated by personal examples from my thirty-five years of feeding on Jesus. I pray that not only will you gain insight into Jesus' metaphor, but also that the actual life of Christ will form in you. If your soul is insatiably crying out, "I'm so hungry for the life of Christ!" then read on, but prepare to lay down the book at times and just feed on Jesus. My hope for you is not more knowledge but a greater measure of the life of Christ formed within you.

Many Christians, especially in the west, are spiritually malnourished but unaware of it. Perhaps we are failing to thrive because we have over-indulged on spiritual substitutes with little nutritional value. Local churches offer a smorgasbord of options intended to feed the soul: need-centered programming, relationships, social activities, varieties of entertaining music and a never-ending stream of biblical information through pulpits, Bible studies, elective classes and online links. But no method, program or tradition within the smorgasbord of religion will ever satisfy the soul or form Christ within. Even doctrinally astute Christians who precisely articulate and defend theology may fail to thrive spiritually, because knowledge of good food does not nourish; consuming it does. The mind can be fed while the soul remains malnourished. Jesus taught us to feed on something greater than knowledge or doctrine - HIMSELF.

There is one indispensable thing neither this book nor any church or person can do for the hungry soul—chew and swallow. Someone else can prepare a meal and even spoon-feed the one at the table, but no one else can chew or swallow for that person. Without commitment to chew and swallow, there is no feeding, no nourishment and no life of Christ formed within. You are reading this book because you've identified a hunger in your soul—something is missing. God wants to form the life of his Son in you and only the Spirit of God can do that. But you must realize no one else, not even God, will chew or swallow for you.

10

This book will offer some suggestions, but it is up to you to initiate ingestion of the life of Christ by feeding on him. As you learn what consuming Christ means, prepare to lay the book down, stop reading and feed on Jesus. Feeding on Jesus requires some understanding, but, above all, practice. Infants learn to feed over time. The book presents opportunities to get you started feeding but it's up to you to learn the skill and, once you've started, to continue. The Lord Jesus himself will instruct your heart and guide you into a deep, nourishing experience of feeding on him.

Think of what you are about to read as principles of spiritual consumption. Once you've learned the principles, personalize them and develop your own unique "feeding style." Learn to feed on Jesus and begin to experience the spiritual satisfaction that comes from consuming Christ as his life forms within you. Go slowly through this book and savor Christ as you go, just as you would an expensive five course meal—enjoy every morsel of Jesus Christ. As you ingest Jesus, his life will form and shape within you until your soul is fully satisfied in him.

In the first chapter, we'll study how Jesus, broken and poured out to be our spiritual food, is the central theme of all scripture. This chapter will help you identify your spiritual hunger and how that hunger can be satisfied completely through consuming Christ as revealed in both the Old and New Testaments.

My dear friend Mary was slender most of her life, but in the nursing home her enlarged abdomen reflected the insatiable feeding of her last days. Her obsessive feeding changed her. May the life of Christ form in you and change you from the inside out as you feed on him.

A Prayer of Swallowing from A. W. Tozer

"O God, I have tasted Thy Goodness, and it has both satisfied me and made me thirsty for more. I am painfully conscious of my need of further grace. I am ashamed of my lack of desire, O God, the Triune God, I want to want Thee; I long to be filled with longing; I thirst to be made more thirsty still. Show me Thy glory, I pray Thee, that so I may know Thee indeed. . . . " (Tozer 20)

QUESTIONS FOR THOUGHT AND INTERACTION
Introduction

1. How is feeding on Jesus like eating a meal?

2. What's the hardest thing about being hungry, both physically and spiritually?

3. What do you think is involved in "eating" Jesus' flesh and "drinking" his blood?

4. Explain how feeding is believing.

5. What keeps us from feeding on Jesus?

6. How will you intentionally contemplate John 6:57?

7. Why is feeding on Jesus necessary for the life of Christ to form within a believer?

Chapter 1
The Table is Set: Jesus, Broken and Poured Out

"Jesus took bread, gave thanks and broke it . . . saying, 'Take and eat; this is my body. Drink from it . . . This is the blood of the covenant which is poured out for many'" (Matthew 26:26-28)

The internal formation of the life of Christ will not happen without a believing response to the gospel. The gospel is not just information to be read and accepted, but the life of Christ to be consumed and formed. Jesus was broken and poured out as a sacrifice of atonement and as spiritual food to be ingested. His sacrifice paid for our sins and when we consume that sacrifice through believing, (feeding), his life takes shape within us. In a sermon from Galatians 4 John Piper said:

> The biblical quest for spiritual formation is a quest to be so shaped from within by the presence of the living Christ that we are no longer 'conformed to this age but are *transformed* by the renewal of our mind' (Romans 12:1, 2); to be so shaped by our union with him that 'the life of Jesus may be manifested in our bodies' (2 Corinthians 4:10); to be so formed and dominated by Christ that we must say with Paul after a life of labor, 'It was not I but the grace of God which is with me' (1 Corinthians 15:10). 'It is no longer I who live but Christ who lives in me' (Galatians 2:20). 'I will not venture to speak of anything except what Christ has wrought through me (Romans 15:18). (Piper, "O, That Christ Would be Formed in You!")

Paul was passionate for the life of Christ to be formed in believing Gentiles. "God has chosen to make known among the Gentiles the glorious riches of this mystery, which is Christ in you, the hope of glory. . . . To this end I labor, struggling with all his energy, which so powerfully works in me" (Col. 1:27, 29). And in Galatians 4:19, Paul said he labored as in the pains of childbirth until Christ was formed in the Galatians. Paul's

13

prayers for believers affirmed this passion for the life of Christ to be formed in them. In Ephesians 3, Paul asked God to strengthen Ephesian believers with power through his Spirit in their inner being. The word "strengthen" in this context means to "increase in vigor." Feeding on the Holy Spirit of Jesus increases spiritual vigor and vitality as the Spirit forms the life of Christ within, "so that Christ may dwell in your hearts through faith" (Eph. 3:17a). The word "dwell" in Paul's prayer of intercession means "to house permanently" and comes from a root word meaning "to occupy or cohabit." A believing response to the gospel, consuming Christ, is the beginning of the life of Christ being formed within the human soul by the power of the Holy Spirit.

God was passionate for his life to dwell in humans from our very inception because he created us in his image. By his foreknowledge, God knew we would fall into sin and require redemption for his life to be fully formed in humans. God would have to provide that redemption and grow his life back into his creatures - the essence of the gospel. The metanarrative of scripture proclaims Jesus Christ as the only spiritual food that is able to impart and sustain life. The entire Bible, both Old and New Testaments, presents the gospel of Jesus Christ as the only hope of the life of God being formed in the human soul. Because this gospel of Jesus Christ was revealed in the Old Testament, there is much we can learn about responding to and consuming Christ from the Old Testament, as New Testament writers declared.

Paul speaks of this Old Testament gospel revelation in Romans 1:1-3, "The gospel he promised beforehand through his prophets in the Holy Scriptures regarding his Son." Peter also references the Old Testament prophets who spoke of future salvation in Christ, "Concerning this salvation, the prophets, who spoke of the grace that was to come to you, searched intently and with the greatest care, trying to find out the time and circumstances to which the Spirit of Christ in them was pointing when he predicted the sufferings of Christ and the glories that would follow" (1 Pet. 1:10-11). All scripture points to Christ, and the very Spirit of Christ inspired the Old Testament prophets to write about the gospel Jesus would bring. Peter proclaimed this in his first sermon, "This is how God fulfilled what he had foretold through all the prophets, saying that his Christ would suffer" (Acts 3:18) and also in his second sermon, found in Acts 3:24.

Paul followed the pattern of Peter's early sermons and used the Old Testament scriptures to explain and prove that the Christ had to suffer and rise from the dead. He proclaimed Jesus as the fulfillment of messianic prophecies in the Old Testament (Acts 17:2-3). Paul told Timothy it was the holy scriptures (Old Testament) that were able to make him wise for salvation through faith in Christ (2 Tim. 3:15). Paul summarized the purpose of the Old Testament to the Galatians in 3:24, "So then, law was put in charge to lead us to Christ that we might be justified by faith." The entire theme of scripture, both Old and New Testaments, is Jesus Christ and the declaration of his gospel.

Jesus himself gave us the greatest assurance of this single theme of scripture while trying to convince the Jews that the Old Testament testified about him: "You diligently study the Scriptures (Old Testament) because you think that by them you possess eternal life. These are the Scriptures that testify about me, yet you refuse to come to me to have life. . . If you believed Moses, you would believe me, for he wrote about me. But since you do not believe what he wrote, how are you going to believe what I say?" (John 5:39-40, 46-47). The Old Testament declares the Christ and points forward to the coming of Christ incarnate, Jesus. Philip recognized this from the first moment he followed Jesus, "We have found the one Moses wrote about in the Law, and about whom the prophets also wrote—Jesus of Nazareth" (John 1:45). Jesus left no doubt about this matter of his gospel being revealed in the Old Testament when he infuriated the Jews in John 8:56 and 58 by saying, "Your father Abraham rejoiced at the thought of seeing my day; he saw it and was glad. . . I tell you the truth, before Abraham was born, I am!"

Immediately following his resurrection, Jesus began to explain what was said about him in the Old Testament so his followers could begin to personally appropriate him:

> How foolish you are, and how slow of heart to
> believe all that the prophets have spoken! Did
> not the Christ have to suffer these things and then

15

enter his glory?. . . Everything must be fulfilled that is written about me in the Law of Moses, and the Prophets and the Psalms. . . This is what is written: The Christ will suffer and rise from the dead on the third day, and repentance and forgiveness of sins will be preached in his name to all nations. . . . (Luke 24:25-26, 44, 46-47)

From Jesus' Emmaus Road instruction forward, the gospel would forever be declared as the fulfillment of the Old Testament scriptures. Jesus told those on the road to Emmaus that all scripture pointed to him, not just the law and prophets (Luke 24:27).

In Matthew 22:43, Jesus, referencing Psalm 110, taught that Israel's King David spoke under the inspiration of the Holy Spirit and identified the Christ as his Lord. David knew the Christ of God (whom we know as Jesus) personally and intimately. David called him Lord, his personal master and savior. Peter referenced David's relationship with Jesus Christ in his Day of Pentecost sermon in Acts 2:31 when he said about David, "Seeing what was ahead, he spoke of the resurrection of the Christ, that he was not abandoned to the grave, nor did his body see decay."

I've given a large amount of attention to Old Testament texts that show the gospel continuity of the Biblical Testaments because it is practically significant to our feeding on Jesus, particularly the example of David. But before considering David, there are other parts of the Old Testament that directly teach us to feed on Christ, consistent with what Jesus taught us to do in John 6. These are known in theological circles as "types of Christ" or illustrations prior to the incarnation that point us to Jesus and how we should respond to him.

The entire system of sacrificial worship revealed in the Pentateuch points to Jesus. The blood sacrifices described in the law point us to the greater reality in Christ. Hebrews 10:1 reminds us the primary purpose of those sacrifices was illustrative, "a shadow of the good things that are coming" - the gospel of Jesus. The sacrifices had no other lasting purpose since they themselves were not able to transform the worshipper, "The law is only a shadow of the good things that are coming—not the realities themselves. For this reason it can never, by the same sacrifices repeated endlessly year after year, make perfect those who draw near to worship." (Heb. 10:1) God was never pleased with the blood of bulls and goats (Isa. 1:11). The sacrificial system of worship was only put in charge to lead us to Christ (Gal. 3:24). Jesus is the only atoning sacrifice for our sins. Just like the meat of animals sacrificed for atonement in the Old Testament was eaten by the priests, so Jesus, broken and poured out as our sacrifice of atonement, is to be consumed by believers. The priests didn't just burn the sacrifice, they consumed it.

But perhaps the most relevant Old Testament type of Christ to our study of feeding on Jesus is the Passover lamb. Passover was an annual feast for the Jews commemorating the night when God struck down all the firstborn of Egypt but "passed over" the Israelites who had brushed the blood of the Passover lamb on their doorframes. The significance of the Passover lamb and how the people were to engage with that lamb point us to Christ. This type is rather obvious when one reads Exodus 12 alongside John 6:53-59.

> On the tenth day of this month [first month of their year] each man is to take a lamb [year old males without defect] . . . and slaughter them at twilight. Then they are to take some of the blood and put it on the sides and tops of the doorframes of the houses where they eat the lambs. That same night they are to eat the meat roasted over the fire . . . Do not leave any of it until morning. . . The blood will be a sign for you on the houses where you are; and when I [God] see the blood, I will pass over you. (Exod. 12:3, 6-10, 13)

The blood of the lamb spread on doorframes spared people from death by God's wrath against the sins of Egypt. Without the shedding of blood from a lamb without defect every firstborn would have perished. The lamb's blood points to the blood of Christ shed for atonement that appeased God's wrath against sin. Paul, writing under inspiration of the Holy Spirit, identified Jesus as our Passover lamb (1 Cor. 5:7). But the Israelites were commanded to do something more than spread the blood of the lamb on their doorframes; they were to consume the lamb, "eat the meat . . . Do not leave any of it till morning" (Exod. 12:8, 10).

Feeding on the sanctified lamb points to our need of consuming Christ. Contemporary evangelical instruction accentuates need of the blood of Christ that saves from God's wrath, but fails to emphasize the necessity of feeding on Jesus.

Spiritual life has always been about consuming Christ, as Paul reminded us in 1 Corinthians 10:3-4 when speaking of the Israelites in the desert, "They all ate the same spiritual food and drank the same spiritual drink; for they drank from the spiritual rock that accompanied them, and that rock was Christ." Whether Moses' day or today, salvation has never been about doctrine, obedience to the law, baptism, acceptance of a creed or reciting a simple prayer. These things are important "table settings" if you will, but life has always been in Christ as believers fed on him. The entire scripture teaches and compels us to consume Christ. So why aren't we feeding on Jesus?

Nearly all the Christians I know want to grow. If we trust Jesus' words in John 6:53-59, we must conclude that growth in Christ happens when the very life of Christ is ingested. Jesus himself, broken and poured out, is life; "my flesh is real food and my blood is real drink" (John 6:55). But it seems many Christians look for nutrition elsewhere - a new spiritual dish, recipe or spiritual supplement to get them growing. Many search for a more "relevant" congregation with which to engage, or a better preacher, a more talented praise team or a local church that offers better programs for children. Others search for nutrients in the latest book, worship song or retreat experience. Our nutritional problems are not due to a lack of food variety or presentation but eating too much of the wrong food. Contemporary churches work hard to create new methods of presentation, but the Church in America still seems to be malnourished. Are we feeding on the methods of presentation and neglecting the food itself? Are we eating too much of the wrong food, spiritual junk food? Let's consider several indispensables for a believer to be properly nourished and healthy.

NUTRIENTS - Jesus

My flesh is real food and my blood is real drink. Whoever eats my flesh and drinks my blood remains in me, and I in him. Just as the living

Father sent me and I live because of the Father, so the one who feeds on me will live because of me. This is the bread that came down from heaven. Your forefathers ate manna and died, but he who feeds on this bread will live forever. (John 6:55-58)

Jesus is our spiritual food source; we have no other. We cannot expect spiritual health and vitality without feeding on Jesus. "I tell you the truth, unless you eat the flesh of the Son of Man and drink his blood, you have no life in you" (John 6:53). The disciples found these words of Jesus hard to swallow. "Many of his disciples said, 'This is a hard teaching. Who can accept it?'" (John 6:60). Is that why we don't hear many sermons on this text? Is that why we rarely hear any explanation of feeding on Jesus when we partake of the elements of bread and wine in remembrance of Jesus? If we neglect or minimize Jesus' instruction in John 6:53-59 in any way, we forfeit eternal life: "I tell you the truth, unless you eat the flesh of the Son of Man and drink his blood, you have no life in you" (John 6:53). We have to understand and apply what Jesus meant by this or all is lost. Why haven't we been taught more about consuming Christ? We hear about eternal life and we all long for it, but unless we feed on Jesus we won't have it; there will be no eternal life. "You have no life in you" (John 6:53b). John 6:53-58 is perhaps the clearest description in all of scripture of how to receive eternal life. Those who feed on Jesus have life. Those who do not feed on him do not have life. John said it poignantly in 1 John 5:12, "He who has the Son has life; he who does not have the Son of God does not have life." We gain his life by feeding on him, broken and poured out. It is imperative that we understand and apply what Jesus teaches us in this passage.

The primary thing John 6 teaches is that Jesus himself is spiritual nourishment, not doctrine about Jesus, not symbolism that illustrates Jesus, not history that records Jesus, not metaphors that compare Jesus, not sermons that proclaim Jesus, not books that teach Jesus, not films that portray Jesus, not songs that worship Jesus, but JESUS. Learn sound doctrine, celebrate through symbols, be a student of history, think deeply about metaphors, listen to sermons, read books, watch films and sing songs, but FEED ON JESUS. The actual, essential, life of Christ is our food. Only Jesus himself can nourish. It's not that Jesus gives us nourishment. No, he *is* the nourishment. Without nourishment there can be no life; and without Jesus, there can be no nourishment.

According to John 6:56, when we feed on Jesus we are united with him and he forms in us. Feeding on Jesus is how the life of Christ is formed in us. Galatians 2:20 describes the outcome: "I no longer live but Christ lives in me. The life I live in the body I live by faith in the Son of God, who loved me and gave himself [broken and poured out] for me." Not only was Christ formed in Paul, but Paul dispensed huge amounts of energy to help the life of Christ be formed in others. "My dear children, for whom I am again in the pains of childbirth until Christ is formed in you" (Gal. 4:19). The word "formed" ("morphe") that Paul used means "to form or fashion within resulting in radical alteration," a new creation as Paul said in 2 Corinthians 5:17. This internal transformation is not of the believer's doing but happens as the life of Christ is formed within. "We . . . are being transformed into his likeness with ever-increasing glory, which comes from the Lord, who is the Spirit" (2 Cor. 3:18).

We must learn to feed on Jesus for him to be formed in us. This book is no more the final word about feeding on Jesus than a chef's recipe is the ultimate presentation of a particular culinary delight, but I do prayerfully hope this writing compels serious contemplation of and intentionality to feed on Jesus. I suppose there are as many ways to feed on Jesus as there are recipes and culinary presentations, but don't confuse presentation and recipe with nutrients. Jesus is the food; everything else is just presentation. Meditate on the previously mentioned examples or types of Christ in Old Testament scripture that motivate feeding on Jesus. Ponder how the Passover lamb was prepared, used and consumed. Think about how the desert-dwelling Israelites ingested nourishment from God by seeking, gathering, preparing and feeding on manna. Be encouraged by the provider God who faithfully supplied that manna every day. Jesus is your manna; feed on him.

Spiritual Junk Food

A few words should be said about things we feed on that don't contribute to spiritual vitality or form the life of Christ within us, because many evangelical Christians are feeding on the wrong things. Local churches work hard to find new recipes and methods of presentation to "serve up the scripture." But have churches focused more on recipes and presentation than on equipping people to chew, swallow and digest Jesus? Clever presentations attract people to sample what's being offered. But after sampling at one congregation, do people tend to look for an even more creative presentation down the street? People move from congregation to congregation as they do from restaurant to restaurant, looking for the newest presentation without digesting what has been served. The newest, most creative presentation seems to attract the most attention.

I just clicked on a popular Christian book website and typed in "Bibles." I was directed to a section titled *Bibles and Bible Accessories*. The number in parentheses said there were 26,463 items in that section. How many ways can we package and market the Bible? It seems there are bibles for every sub-culture imaginable, every aesthetic palate and every problem people face. Are we helping people feed on the word or just serving it up on a fancy plate? What are bible accessories anyway, and how many do we need? How many homes in America contain hundreds of dollars' worth of bibles and bible accessories which still look new because no one has really chewed on them? I suppose certain "repackaged bibles" may be effective at stimulating the intellect, but a balanced diet of Jesus nourishes the entire soul and leads to healthy, growing spirituality. The purpose of God's word is not just to increase our knowledge but to reveal and feed us Jesus. Jesus is our food.

Think metaphorically about eating a physical meal compared to feeding on Jesus through the Bible. How silly would it be to sit down at the supper table and intellectually analyze a meal to gain culinary knowledge but never digest the food? It might go something like this: *"The corn kernels look a little small. Was it a dry summer? Perhaps these kernels reflect a particular seed hybrid. Is the nutritional value less or greater than the bigger, lighter colored kernels?"* EAT THE CORN! Imagine cutting into a nice piece of beef and instead of eating it you analyze it by asking: *"Is this grain or pasture fed? Is it properly lean for my dietary needs or should I trim a bit more fat? How many bites should I take to optimize my caloric intake for protein? What would be the optimal number of chewing repetitions to maximize the beginning of the digestive cycle for this piece of meat?"* EAT THE MEAT! Intellectual analysis and presentation without feeding is worthless nutritionally. When I sit at the table for a dinner, there is very little intellectual analysis and a whole lot of, *"Pass the meat and the corn. Is there more bread? What's for dessert?"* I sit at the table to eat. It ought be the same spiritually.

Feeding on Jesus is more than intellectual engagement with the Bible. That's why we need to learn to consume Christ, not just read about him. We don't need more unique bibles or impressive software. We have what we need in Jesus Christ. "Whoever eats my flesh and drinks my blood has eternal life" (John 6:54). The Bible sets the food before us—Jesus broken and poured out for us. We need less presentation (creatively presented bibles) and more consumption, fewer recipes (church programs) and more chewing, less competition amongst restaurants (congregations) and more feeding by the people in the restaurants—the Church.

Soda pop was virtually unheard of until the late 1800's, when Coca-Cola and other variations of soda were created. Take a walk today down the pop aisle of any supermarket. The varieties of soda are staggering. But the combined nutritional value of an entire aisle of soda is insignificant. Soda sells because it appeals to the craving for sugary drink, which has little to do with nutrition. Spiritual sugar water has little nutritional value. Churches that teach how to maximize joy in marriage, manage money, parent children and serve neighbors teach great things. But if in teaching those things a Church neglects the real nutritional need of the soul, we might as well be pushing soda pop—it tastes good but doesn't satisfy nutritionally.

HUNGER - Need for Jesus

A second indispensable for a well-nourished soul, in addition to proper nutrients, is hunger. People who aren't hungry don't eat. People who are just a little bit hungry don't eat much, but a person who hasn't eaten in days feeds much differently. The person with a bottle of water on his desk drinks differently from a construction worker who has labored outside in ninety degree heat. As a toddler, my emotive eldest child often said, "I am starving thirsty!" "Starving thirsty" people drink differently. Hunger and thirst are prerequisites to proper nutritional intake.

But sadly, I don't know many people "starving thirsty" for Jesus. J.C. Ryle, who wrote in the mid to late 1880s, articulated what may be the primary reason for our contemporary lack of hunger for Jesus: "We may depend upon it, men will never come to Jesus, and stay with Jesus, and live for Jesus, unless they really know why they are to come, and what is their need . . . Let him see his sin and he must see his Savior. . . nothing will satisfy him but the great Physician" (Ryle 15, 17). Ryle described a deficient view of human depravity. If people aren't aware of their sin, why would they hunger for Jesus? Psychology, social science and anthropology have convinced our culture that human beings are not inherently sinful or separated from God. The few pockets within culture that still affirm human depravity often fail to grasp the vast chasm sin has entrenched between humans and God.

When I was a youth pastor, I made it a practice to ask teenagers, "Do you believe we are born basically good, evil or neutral?" The unofficial results showed about 95% thought humans are born basically good or neutral. That was thirty years ago, so I would guess the percentage to be even higher now. If we consider ourselves basically good or neutral, we'll think of God as one who exists to meet our needs and expectations like a clerk in a drive-up window. "I need God to bless me but not to save me." If God can somehow overlook my sin and exists primarily to make me happy, why do I need a redeemer? Why would I feed on Jesus when I'm not hungry for him?

The Bible teaches humans are sinful from birth (Ps. 51:5, Gen. 8:21, Rom. 3:23, 7:18) and because of that innate depravity, we stand condemned before God (John 3:18) from the moment of conception. Embracing that truth creates hunger for a savior. We have lost passionate hunger for Jesus Christ because we sense no real urgent need for him. Instead of consuming Christ out of "starving thirst" and desperation, we just nibble and sip when it's convenient and socially acceptable. Without desperate hunger we will not feed on Christ; and if we don't feed on him, we will be malnourished and fail to thrive to eternal life.

In his classic book *Dynamics of Spiritual Life* Richard F. Lovelace said, "Acceptance of Christ is conditioned on awareness of God's holiness and conviction of the depth of our sin. Men and women cannot know themselves until they know the reality of the God who made them, and once they know the holy God, their own sin appears so grievous that they cannot rest until they have fully appropriated Christ" (Lovelace 81, 82). Knowing God revealed in scripture and knowing the depraved, sinful human condition creates an insatiable appetite for Jesus Christ, the only savior. Until we rediscover God biblically and think correctly of ourselves in relation to him, our appetite for Jesus will be minimal.

How will the Church hunger for Christ if preaching fails to proclaim innate sinfulness and God's inflexible holiness? Until Christian literature creates a deep spiritual hunger that only Christ can satisfy instead of more ways to be happy, who will feed on Jesus? Church music that speaks about Jesus as friend and lover but fails to exalt Christ as Savior from sin feeds the entertainment obsession of our culture but does little to nourish salvation. Sermons that speak of human sinfulness don't woo large crowds but they do create spiritual appetite. Books that fail to offer easy, quick fixes aren't best sellers, and music that exalts the savior from sin may not float to the top of the charts, but if Christian leaders fail to create an insatiable hunger for Jesus, Christian people will fail to feed on Jesus.

DIGESTION - Commitment

A third indispensable for proper nutrition is digestion. Without digestion, nutrients are not absorbed into the systems of the body. Digestion is the changing of food, by the action of gastric and intestinal juices, into a form that can be absorbed by the body. The process requires a great amount of the body's energy and attention. There is a digestive process for the soul as well, or Jesus would not have taught us John 6:53-58.

Why then has so much evangelical instruction about eternal life been reduced to the small, one time "bite" of accepting Jesus into my heart? Over the last century in America, belief in Christ has become to many evangelicals nothing more than intellectual agreement with the facts of the gospel, affirmed by a trite prayer that someone else wrote. When someone says he believes in Christ, it may be no more significant than saying he believes Iceland exists. But saving faith is more than just intellectual assent to the facts of the gospel expressed through an impersonal prayer; it is feeding on Jesus. The Apostle James said, "You believe that there is one God. Good! Even the demons believe that" (Jas. 2:19). Demons acknowledge the truth of Christ but do not trust in Christ by feeding on him. Paul said to King Agrippa in Acts 26:27, "I know you believe," but Agrippa showed no evidence of personal trust in Christ.

It is possible to pray a "salvation prayer" that someone else wrote and acknowledge belief in the facts of the gospel without ever placing personal trust in Christ. Nowhere does the Bible teach that belief means simply reciting a prayer someone else wrote. Thousands of spiritually malnourished people wonder why they are still hungry, having been promised satisfaction through one "intellectual bite" of Jesus. Accepting Christ by reciting a prayer someone else wrote is not the conclusion of a faith journey but, at best, the beginning. The evangelical Church has so accentuated this initial acceptance of Jesus that many have made the beginning of faith the end. Saving faith is an ongoing response of consuming Christ that culminates at glorification, not with initial acceptance of Jesus.

People often think of repentance as a one-time thought or truth embraced through reciting a "salvation prayer." But even repentance can be merely intellectual and not an authentic expression of the heart. Paul mentions earnestness of heart in his description of authentic repentance in 2 Corinthians 7:8-11. The Old Testament contains many examples of repentance that did not result in transformation. Transformation occurs not by some new thought to the mind but by a new Spirit in the heart: "I will give you a new heart and put a new spirit in you; I will remove from you your heart of stone and give you a heart of flesh. And I will put my spirit in you and move you to follow my decrees and be careful to keep my laws" (Ezek. 36:26-27). Transformation happens when a new Spirit is injected into the human heart, not when the mind apprehends a new truth. What's new about the new covenant or testament is not repentance but the life of

25

Christ implanted in the believer by the Spirit of Christ.

The Spirit must be digested in the soul of the believer, and this happens when the soul feeds on and swallows Jesus. Chewing and swallowing is a commitment to feed. Until a person places food in the mouth, chews it and swallows it, the final act of digestive commitment, no nutrition is gained. Digestion is "automatic" once food is swallowed, but swallowing requires commitment. Commitment to feed on Jesus creates spiritual vitality as the life of Christ takes shape within and begins to bear fruit.

Jesus taught in the Sermon on the Mount, "By their fruit you will recognize them" (Matt. 7:16a). Fruit is the outcome of plants absorbing water and nutrients—if you will, the plant's "digestion." Why are there so many fruitless Christians? Perhaps it is because so few Christians are absorbing or consuming Christ. The glaring need of Christians in America is to feed on Jesus, and feeding requires commitment. Jesus' metaphor of the vine and branches in John 15 teaches us digestive commitment. "No branch can bear fruit by itself; it must remain in the vine." (John 15:4). Fruitful Christians bear fruit because they are committed to feeding off the vine of Christ. The branch receives nutrition as the nourishing sap flows from vine to branch. If that branch is separated from the vine so that it can no longer "swallow" the nourishing sap it will die. It is impossible for a dead branch to bear fruit separated from the vine. Realize also, that a branch doesn't just feed once, but continually through the enduring commitment of vine to branch and branch to vine—a blessed union that enables the flow of life-giving sap, resulting in fruit. "If you remain in me and my words remain you, ask whatever you wish, and it will be given you. This is to my Father's glory, that you bear much fruit" (John 15:7-8). Connection to the vine is commitment to an organic union that enables continuous feeding from the vine and continuous consumption by the branch. Without life-giving sap from the vine, no fruit will ever grow on the branch. In such a case, the branch is cut off (John 15:2).

EXERCISE - Mission

One final indispensable for spiritual vitality is proper exercise.

Christian mission, properly executed, is exercise that keeps Christians spiritually fit. Mission is the natural outgrowth of a properly nourished soul in which the life of Christ is forming. The more Christians are on mission, the greater their hunger for Christ. I experience this outcome every time I exercise physically. I know it's important to be fit and manage my weight, but when I exercise I get hungry, really hungry! Sometimes exercise becomes almost counterproductive as a strategy for managing weight because I end up digesting more calories than I worked off in order to satisfy my hunger. I love to eat, and the more I exercise, the more I want to eat. The more I eat, the more I need exercise to burn off those unwanted calories, and then my appetite gets even more ferocious. This cycle is not so helpful for physical fitness but great for spiritual fitness, because the more I live on mission the more I hunger to consume Christ.

Properly executed, mission for Christ compels feeding on Jesus. The more the soul feeds on Jesus, the more the soul serves Jesus, creating even more hunger. That cycle nourishes spiritual health and fitness. Christ does not form himself in believers to make them fat but to transform believers, who can then transform culture around them. "Missional exercise" keeps us lean and healthy. The life of Christ digested becomes the energy of Christian mission. The more I consume Christ, the more the life of Christ is formed in me; and the more Christ is formed in me, the more Christ's mission extends from me. Consuming Christ is indispensable for Christian ministry and leadership.

Embrace all the creative spiritual recipes and presentation you want, but remember to consume Christ. Only Jesus Christ is spiritual nourishment. Garnish, sauces, presentation or an impressive plate doesn't nourish, only Jesus. Self-improvement, emotion or a bite here or there doesn't nourish. We're spiritually malnourished because we don't feed or we feed on the wrong food. We need to consume Christ. Learn to ingest the actual presence and life of Christ.

The last words of Jesus' great prayer of intercession for the church in John 17:26 help us understand the Lord's desire for us. In the last part of the prayer, Jesus asks for a special kind of union between himself and the Church, "that all of them may be one, Father, just as you are in me and I am in you" (John 17:21).

27

This union is deeper and more essential than we think. It is more profound than simply having knowledge or the influence of Jesus. It is his actual presence dwelling within believers, "I have made you known to them, and will continue to make you known in order that the love you have for me may be in them and that I myself may be in them" (John 17:26). Jesus doesn't just want his love to dwell in us, but the very essence of his being. That is why he taught us to feed on him, and why he was broken and poured out for us. The table has been set. Learn to consume Christ.

Chapter 2 will present how King David of Israel nourished his soul by feeding on Christ. Four key activities of consuming Christ emerge from a study of the psalms David wrote. But David's example is insufficient because Jesus had not yet been broken and poured out. Now that Jesus has been broken and poured out, we have a greater invitation and opportunity to feed on him than David had. Follow David's example to lead you to Jesus, but pursue more than knowing Jesus; feed on him.

QUESTIONS FOR THOUGHT AND INTERACTION
Chapter 1

1. Why is Jesus' being broken and poured out significant for consuming Christ?

2. What Old Testament "types" of Jesus most help you understand the process of consuming Christ?

3. How is John 6:53 encouraging? How is it scary?

4. How does consuming Christ help form the life of Christ in a feeding believer?

5. Describe some spiritual "junk food" that gives your soul a short-term spiritual high?

6. How is proper spiritual digestion different from a one-time bite of accepting Jesus?

Chapter 2
David's Instructive but Insufficient Example

"The Spirit of the Lord spoke through me; his word was on my tongue"
(2 Samuel 23:2)

God taught the prophet Samuel, who was searching for a king to replace Saul, that a heart for God was more important for leadership than appearance, height or other outward features (1 Sam. 16:7). As the Lord looked upon the heart of a young shepherd, he found "David son of Jesse a man after my own heart" (Acts 13:22). David was an extraordinary Old Testament character whose heart for God was perhaps his most distinctive characteristic. "Heart," when used in biblical contexts like this one, refers to the center of the mind, will and emotions. David pursued God holistically—with his mind, will and emotions. David fed his mind with thoughts of God, his choices with the will of God and nourished his emotions with the passions of God. But how can David, an Old Testament character, be an instructive example for us to feed on Jesus? Christ forms his life in our hearts as we consume him. The heart is the gastro-intestinal system of the spiritual life. It is from the Spirit of Christ forming in the human heart that the life of Christ is disseminated throughout. The stomach and intestines absorb nutrition from food into the bloodstream. The heart absorbs nutrition from the indwelling Spirit of Christ into the lifeblood of the soul, forming Christ throughout.

David's psalms are a window into his heart for God. David is more transparent with his heart than any other character of scripture. The words of David's psalms are personal and intimate expressions of his passionate engagement with God. Therefore, his writings are most instructive about how to feed the heart with the life of Christ. How can David, who lived hundreds of years before the incarnation of Jesus, instruct us in feeding on Jesus? Remember from Chapter one that Jesus is revealed in all of scripture. David responded to that revelation personally and passionately expressed his response like no one else in the Old Testament.

David knew Jesus personally. He did not address him as Jesus and couldn't have imagined what all his Christ would accomplish when he came in the flesh, but David knew Jesus personally, even intimately. David's psalms are intimate expressions between David and his Lord, a window into a profound relationship David had with the second person of the Godhead. David's words in Psalm 110:1 (both Jesus and Peter quoted them in the New Testament) remove all doubt about this incredible relationship David had with the Lord Jesus. In Psalm 110:1 David says, "The LORD says to my Lord." The first use of the word LORD in this verse is upper case letters, a translation of the title Jehovah, or "self-existent one" in Hebrew. The second use of the word Lord is lower case letters, Adonai in Hebrew, meaning "Lord or master." So the text reads, "Jehovah says to my Adonai," apparently a reference to two distinct persons within the Trinitarian God. This would not be true if David were just addressing God by two different titles, as he appears to do in Psalm 8:1, "O LORD, our Lord, how majestic is your name in all the earth!" But in Psalm 110:1 Jehovah speaks to Adonai, so these titles must refer to two persons of the Trinity engaged in some type of communication.

Jesus referenced this remarkable passage in dialogue with the Pharisees, as recorded by Matthew in Chapter 22 of his gospel. Jesus asked the Pharisees whose son they thought the Christ or Messiah was. They said, "The son of David." Jesus responded, "How is it then that David, speaking by the Holy Spirit, calls him 'Lord'?" (Matt. 22:43). Jesus then quoted Psalm 110:1 to help the Pharisees understand that David addressed the Messiah as his personal Lord, Adonai. Jesus taught that Adonai, referenced by David in Psalm 110:1, was indeed a reference to the Messiah, who had now come and was speaking to them—Jesus. David personally knew Christ Jesus as his Lord, the one in control of his life, his master.

Peter incorporated this same text from Psalm 110 into the sermon he preached on the day of Pentecost after the Holy Spirit had been poured out. Peter, referring to David, said,

> He was a prophet and knew that God had promised him on oath that he would place one of his descendants on his throne. Seeing what was

ahead, he [David] spoke of the resurrection of the Christ, that he was not abandoned to the grave, nor did his body see decay. . . For David did not ascend to heaven, and yet he said, "The Lord said to my Lord: Sit at my right hand until I make your enemies a footstool for your feet." (Acts 2:30-35)

David knew Jesus personally and intimately because, by faith, he was looking ahead to the things promised (Heb. 11:13).

DAVID'S PSALMS - An example of intimacy

David's psalms are, therefore, an exemplary window into an intimate relationship between Christ the Lord and a man after God's heart—the most intimate examples of interpersonal interaction between God and man recorded in the scripture. Even though David addressed God much more often in his psalms by the title Jehovah, (LORD in the New International Version of the Bible), his uses of Adonai, (Lord in the New International Version of the Old Testament), demonstrate he understood something of Trinitarian theology. David had an intimately personal relationship with the second person of the Trinity, as the psalms he wrote demonstrate. This compilation of David's psalms expresses the close relationship David enjoyed with the Lord:

> But you are a shield around me, O Lord; you bestow glory on me and lift up my head. (Psa. 3:3) I will lie down and sleep in peace, for you alone, O Lord, make me dwell in safety. (Psa. 4:8) In the morning, O Lord, you hear my voice; in the morning I lay my requests before you and wait in expectation. (Psa. 5:3) Those who know your name will trust in you, for you, Lord, have never forsaken those who seek you. (Psa. 9:10) I will sing to the Lord, for he has been good to me. (Psa. 13:6) I said to the LORD, 'You are my Lord; apart from you I have no good thing.' (Psa. 16:2) Some trust in chariots and some in horses, but we trust in the name of the Lord our God. (Psa. 20:7) O Lord, the king rejoices in your strength. (Psa. 21:1a) Do not be far from me; for

trouble is near and there is no one to help. (Psa. 22:11) . . . You are with me; your rod and your staff, they comfort me. (Psa. 23:4) Test me, O Lord, and try me, examine my heart and my mind; . . .(Psa. 26:2) The Lord is my light and my salvation—whom shall I fear? The Lord is the stronghold of my life - of whom shall I be afraid? (Psa. 27:1) Into your hands I commit my spirit; . . . (Psa. 31:5) Then I acknowledged my sin to you and did not cover up my iniquity. (Psa. 32:5) The angel of the Lord encamps around those who fear him, and he delivers them. (Psa. 34:7) Delight yourself in the Lord and he will give you the desires of your heart. (Psa. 37:4)

In Psalm 139, David says God knows him well enough to know when he sits and when he rises, when he goes out and when he lies down, even his words before David speaks them. David declares that wherever he goes, God is present with him to guide and hold him fast. In verse 17, David says, "How precious to me are your thoughts, O God!" (Psalm 139:17a). He loved God with all his heart. David trusted so much in God's loving kindness that he even asked God to search his heart, to test him and know his anxious thoughts. He petitioned God to investigate if there was any offensive way in David and to then lead David in the way everlasting. This man knew Christ intimately.

David expressed profound dependence in the Lord in Psalms 51-64 and 69-70, all written when David was in some kind of trouble. When trouble came, David cried out to the Lord for help:

Save me, O God, by your name. . . . (Ps. 54:1a) He has delivered me from all my troubles, and my eyes have looked in triumph on my foes. (Ps. 54:7) Cast your cares on the Lord. . . . (Ps. 55:22a) When I am afraid, I will trust in you. (Ps. 56:3) I cry out to God Most High. . . . (Ps. 57:2a) . . . deliver me from my enemies, O God. . . . (Ps. 59:1) Find rest, O my soul, in God alone; . . . (Ps.

33

62:5) O God, you are my God, earnestly I seek you; my soul thirsts for you, my body longs for you, in a dry and weary land where there is no water. (Ps. 63:1) . . . I am poor and needy; come quickly to me, O God. (Ps. 70:5a)

The relationship between David and Jesus Christ was so intimate that the Spirit of Jesus even spoke through David in what are called Messianic Psalms. David himself understood this, "The Spirit of the LORD spoke through me; his word was on my tongue" (2 Sam. 23:2). Jesus acknowledged it in Matthew 22:43, "David, speaking by the Spirit. . ." and the New Testament believers declared it, "You spoke by the Holy Spirit through the mouth of your servant, our father David" (Acts 4:25a). In the Messianic psalms, the Lord Jesus actually speaks through the mouth of David by the Holy Spirit. At times, the very life of Christ was speaking through David.

Psalm 22 is a profound example of David speaking by the Holy Spirit and articulating the heart of Jesus as he hung on the cross:

My God, my God, why have you forsaken me? All who see me mock me; they hurl insults, shaking their heads. He trusts in the Lord. . . let the Lord rescue him. Let him deliver him, since he delights in him. . . . I am poured out like water, and all my bones are out of joint. My heart has turned to wax; it has melted away within me. . . . They have pierced my hands and feet. . . . They divide my garments among them and cast lots for my clothing. (Ps. 22:1a, 7-8, 14, 16b, 18)

These very words and thoughts of Jesus from the cross were penned by David hundreds of years before the Lord ever spoke them. David's cries to God for help in Psalm 69 expressed Jesus' cry for help from the cross, "The insults of those who insult you fall on me. . . . They put gall in my food and gave me vinegar for my thirst" (Ps. 69:9b, 21).

I first learned about having a personal relationship with Jesus Christ as an eight-year-old child. People who had a relationship with Christ taught and modeled for me how to develop such a relationship. Years later, I remember one teacher challenged me by saying, "A lot of people have a relationship with the Church or with Christians, but not so many have a relationship with Jesus Christ." I began to read all I could about developing a personal relationship with Jesus. It was during that season that God opened the psalms of David to my heart. I fell in love with David's heart because his heart for God taught me how to love Jesus. I've learned more about relational intimacy with Jesus from David, who lived hundreds of years before Jesus came in the flesh, than from any other source. I've learned four key principles of relational engagement with Jesus from studying David's psalms: Ponder, Pour Out, Petition and Praise.

PONDER - to think deeply about

"All mankind will fear; they will proclaim the works of God and ponder what he has done" (Ps. 64:9). David used the word "ponder" to describe his deep thoughts of God, as did other writers of the psalms: "Great are the works of the Lord; they are pondered by all who delight in them" (Ps. 111:2). This deep thinking about God was vital to David, who spent so much time running for his life from Saul and other enemies. Psalm 63, written by David from the desert of Judah, expresses a desperate thirst for God, "O God, you are my God, earnestly I seek you; my soul thirsts for you, my body longs for you, in a dry and weary land where there is no water" (Ps. 63:1). To satisfy his thirst, David ponders God: "I have seen you in the sanctuary and beheld your power and your glory. . . . Your love is better than life. . . . On my bed I remember you; I think of you through the watches of the night" (Ps. 63:2-3a, 6). Pondering God brought satisfaction to David's soul. "My soul will be satisfied as with the richest of foods" (Ps. 63:5).

In other, more peaceful times, David is gazing into the heavens, which prompts deep thoughts of God, "When I consider your heavens, the work of your fingers, the moon and the stars, which you have set in place, what is man that you are mindful of him" (Ps. 8:3-4a) and "The heavens declare the glory of God; the skies proclaim the work of his hands" (Ps. 19:1). These deep thoughts of God compelled David to praise God (Ps. 8:1, 9). On another occasion, David was apparently reminiscing while pondering God, "I remember the days of long ago; I

35

meditate on all your works and consider what your hands have done" (Ps. 143:5). Pondering God was a regular practice of David in all kinds of circumstances.

And why not? Would we expect less of an intimate relationship? Does not a lover think often of his beloved? Does the object of one's significant affection not occupy much of his thinking? Those who love God think about God. Those who think about God are nourished in their souls because of pondering God. In addition to pondering God, (Chapter 3 presents more on pondering), David related intimately with God through another common experience of those who relate intimately - pouring out his heart.

POUR OUT

A person will rarely bare his heart to another person, and never without profound trust and confidence in that other person. David had that kind of trust in the Lord. "Trust in him at all times, O people; pour out your hearts to him, for God is our refuge" (Ps. 62:8). Because David pondered the character and goodness of God, he trusted him enough to pour out his heart to God. People pour out their souls to a select few. Wives pour out to their husbands or close friends, but rarely to children. Men pour out to . . . Ok, men rarely pour out their hearts to anyone; but David was different, and his relationship with God was different—characterized, among other things, by David's pouring out his heart. "I cry aloud to the Lord; I lift up my voice to the Lord for mercy. I pour out my complaint before him; before him I tell my trouble" (Ps. 142:1-2). David knew God intimately enough to complain to him, to express anger and fear to him. He let God know about his troubles - the relational intimacy of pouring out one's heart to another.

PRAISE

David used the word "praise" in relation to God nearly eighty times in his psalms, depending on the version of scripture. Psalms 122, 124, 131, 133, 144 and 145 are all attributed to David as songs of ascent (sung while marching victoriously) or praise. I will cite many more examples of praise in Chapter 8, but for now, this is a simple reminder that we praise what we love and adore.

Praise is verbalized affection or audible compliments. We praise people we love, admire and adore.

PETITION

The fourth "P" modeled by David is petitioning the Lord. "Petition" means "a specific ask," something people aren't comfortable doing. When people verbalize neediness, it's usually to close friends or family. David asked God for all kinds of things. He was not bashful to petition the one he loved:

> One thing I ask of the Lord, this is what I seek . . . . In the morning, O Lord, you hear my voice; in the morning I lay my requests before you and wait in expectation. Do not rebuke me in your anger or discipline me in your wrath. Be merciful to me, Lord, for I am faint; O Lord, heal me, for my bones are in agony. . . . . Let the light of your face shine upon us, O Lord. (Ps. 27:4a, 5:3, 6:1-2, 4:6b)

David petitioned often, but one thing David never petitioned was the life of Christ to dwell within him. David did experience some presence of the Spirit, as has already been pointed out, but not the indwelling of Christ. David did not have the opportunity to consume Christ that believers have today.

So, while David's intimate expressions are helpful for us in developing a relationship, God desires more for us. God doesn't just want to walk and talk with us, as wonderful as that is. God doesn't long only to be our friend or to have a love relationship with us. He has something even more incredible than a personal relationship in mind for believers in Christ. It is not something David, nor any of the Old Testament characters, had, because it was not available to them. David, as intimate as he was with the Lord, did not have opportunity to have what we have, the life of Christ indwelling and being formed within. The gospel is greater than relationship—it is union with Christ; it is Christ becoming greater and the believer becoming less; it is Christ in you, the hope of glory. Union with Christ transcends relationship. My most intimate relationship is with my beautiful wife of thirty-five years, but she is not in me and I am not in her. Have we sold the gospel short by marketing its greatest value as a relationship of companionship, friendship and lover? Jesus Christ is companion, friend and lover to believers, but so much more.

There is not one occurrence in David's psalms where he petitioned the Spirit to dwell within him. It probably never occurred to David to ask, since the Spirit had not been given because Jesus had not yet been glorified. Psalm 51:11 is as close as David comes to petitioning the Spirit of Jesus, "Do not cast me from your presence or take your Holy Spirit from me" (Ps. 51:11). David was aware of the Spirit's presence, but not in the indwelling way New Testament believers experienced. Hebrews 11:13, which includes David, says, "All these people were still living by faith when they died. They did not receive the things promised; they only saw them and welcomed them from a distance." And later in the chapter, "They were all commended for their faith, yet none of them received what had been promised. God had planned something better for us so that only together with us would they be made perfect" (Heb. 11:39-40). This is the shocking reality of the gospel—the Old Testament greats did not receive it in full because it was not available to them. They longed for something more and tried to figure out what it might be, as Peter taught in his first letter:

> Concerning this salvation, the prophets, who spoke of the grace that was to come to you, searched intently and with the greatest care, trying to find out the time and circumstances to which the Spirit of Christ in them was pointing when he predicted the sufferings of Christ and the glories that would follow. It was revealed to them that they were not serving themselves but you, when they spoke of the things that have now been told you by those who have preached the gospel to you by the Holy Spirit sent from heaven. Even angels long to look into these things.
> (1 Pet. 1:10-12)

These three texts from John 7, Hebrews 11 and 1 Peter 1, remind New Testament believers about the unique privilege of the indwelling Holy Spirit, sent in the name of Jesus to form the life of Christ within us. This is a privilege Old Testament greats did not have.

The Holy Spirit "came upon" people in the Old Testament, but not in the way of New Testament gospel. The Spirit spoke through Old Testament prophets, as the New Testament texts teach us. God used the intimate relationship with David to speak through him (2 Sam. 23:2) and other prophets, but the Spirit did not indwell them in the gospel way. In the Old Testament, the Spirit is said to "be among you" (Hag. 2:5) or more often, to "come upon." The description of the Spirit that "comes" or "came upon" is written of Moses and seventy elders of Israel, Balaam, Judges, Othniel, Gideon, Jephthah, Samson, King Saul, his men and the kings David, Amasai, Azariah, Jahaziel, Zechariah and prophets Joel and Ezekiel. This "coming upon" appeared to be a circumstantial empowerment for particular tasks or responsibilities given by God, but does not appear to have been an ongoing internal presence. In the Old Testament, the Spirit works providentially and powerfully through people, but not to shape or form the life of God internally, as is the case with the gospel. The New Testament tells a very different story of the Holy Spirit.

NEW TESTAMENT PRESENCE OF HOLY SPIRIT

Following his resurrection and ascension, Jesus promised something totally new to his followers, the indwelling presence of the Holy Spirit (John 14:16-17). This Holy Spirit would not only be upon them, as he was with many in the Old Testament, but would also form himself within them. Jesus promised the Holy Spirit would teach them (John 14:26), reveal truth to them and guide them in that truth (John 16:13-15) and form himself in them, "for he lives with you and will be in you" (John 14:17b). This indwelling Spirit of Christ is unique to New Testament believers and is likely the promise to which Hebrews 11:13 and 39a refers, ". . . they did not receive the things promised . . . These were all commended for their faith, yet none of them received what had been promised." Jesus said that on the day the promise was fulfilled, "you will realize that I am in my Father, and you are in me, and I am in you" (John 14:20). The last words of Jesus' great prayer of intercession for the church in John 17:26b were, "that I myself may be in them." It is the Father's will and the Son's passionate desire to be formed in believers by

39

the promised gift of the indwelling Spirit.

Other New Testament writers also recognized the indwelling Spirit as fulfillment of the promise. Peter recognized the giving of the Holy Spirit in Acts 2:16-17 as the promise, "this is what was spoken by the prophet Joel: 'In the last days . . . I will pour out my Spirit on all people.'" Paul speaks of being filled with the Spirit throughout his letters: Romans 8:9-11, 1 Corinthians 3:16,19, Galatians 4:6, 19, Colossians 1:27. To his disciple in the Lord, Timothy, Paul said, "Guard the good deposit that was entrusted to you—guard it with the help of the Holy Spirit who lives in us" (2 Tim. 1:14). John speaks of it in his letters as well, "the one who is in you is greater than the one who is in the world" (1 John 4:4).

The result of this fulfilled promise to which the Old Testament points and the New Testament testifies is, "so that the life of Jesus may also be revealed in our body" (2 Cor. 4:11b). This is God's goal for believers - transformation. God wants to so form Christ in us that through us the life of Jesus will be revealed in our very bodies! This is the work of the gospel within, but if we reduce belief to intellectual agreement with the facts of the gospel, expressed only by the recitation of a prayer someone else wrote, how will the life of Christ be formed within us? Paul said it is by faith that we receive this promise of the Spirit which forms Christ in us (Gal. 3:14b). Couple this with Jesus' instruction in John 6:53-59, (feeding is believing), and we may conclude that to feed on Jesus is to continually receive his Spirit, which forms the very life of Christ in believers. This is the life of Christ in the soul of man. This is Christ in you, the hope of glory. This is why Paul expended the energy of childbirth, "until Christ is formed in you" (Gal. 4:19b).

As Christ takes form within believers, fruit of that life will develop. Again Jesus' metaphor of the vine and the branches provides insight into this organic development of the Spirit filling and flowing through believers to produce fruit of the Spirit. John wedged that instructive metaphor into his gospel in the middle of Jesus' promise and instruction about the Spirit in John Chapters 14 and 16. Branches connected to the vine receive their fullness of life from the sap that flows to them through the vine. So the life of Christ is formed in "feeding" believers as the Holy Spirit of Christ flows to them through the vine of Christ. Fruit of the Spirit develops not due to some work of the branch, but because the life of the vine flows through the branch. The only work the branch must do is to stay connected to the vine and continue receiving the sap that flows through the vine. I feel sorry for David and the other Old Testament heroes of faith. Had the Holy Spirit been available to fill those believers, they certainly would have asked for it as we are commanded to do by Paul in Ephesians 5:18 and by Jesus himself in Luke 11:13b, "How much more will your Father in heaven give the Holy Spirit to those who ask him!" The New Testament closes with this great gospel invitation to all people to drink in the Spirit of Christ, what the ancients could not receive because Jesus had not yet been glorified: "The Spirit and the bride say 'Come!' And let him who hears say, 'Come!' Whoever is thirsty, let him come; and whoever wishes, let him take the free gift of the water of life" (Rev. 22:17). By the atonement, invitation and power of Jesus Christ the Holy Spirit will indwell those who believe and ask to be filled. This is the beginning of the life of Christ being formed within—the transformative power of the gospel.

Why then do we settle for friendship with Jesus, as wonderful as that is? Why be content with an external relationship with Jesus when he can dwell within you and change you from the inside out? Why love Jesus without embracing the forming of his life within you? Why do we write songs of passionate love and friendship to Jesus but petition him so little about forming his life within us? Why do we pursue Jesus "walking and talking with us" as the end of our faith, instead of the beginning of his life growing to maturity within us? As wonderful as it would be to have Jesus sitting next to me, walking with me, teaching me and leading me by the hand, is it not better to have Jesus forming within me, changing me into his likeness from the core of my heart outward? Maybe we just want his friendship and not the life he wants to form in us. We want him to befriend, encourage and affirm our lives without our fully embracing his life transforming us from the inside out. "We live in a narcissistic culture, and it's easy to turn God into a supporting actor in our life movie rather than be swept into His story of redemption" (*Gospel-Driven Life* 70). Paul did not say the hope of glory is walking hand in hand with Jesus on a beach but "Christ in you, the hope of glory" (Col. 1:27b). John didn't say we know Jesus walks beside us as a faithful companion, but "this is how we know he lives in us: we know it by the Spirit he gave us. . . . We know . . . that he lives in us, because he has given us of his Spirit" (1 John 3:24b, 4:13). Jesus prayed to the Father about being formed in us, (John 17:21); he didn't ask for the privilege of being our buddy. Yes, we can call Jesus our friend, (John 15:13-15) but he has so much more for us.

To "accept Jesus" as my Savior without dying to my own life and embracing his life forming within me not only is unbiblical but also totally ignores the transformational reality of the gospel. God wants you to know him intimately, as David did, but he has and wants more for you. He wants to form the life of Christ in you. Paul prayed for the Ephesians that Christ would strengthen them with power through his Spirit in their inner being, so that Christ might dwell in their hearts through faith (Eph. 3:16-17). He commanded the Romans to be transformed by the renewing of their minds, (Rom. 12:2) but taught them this would only happen as they presented their bodies to Jesus as living sacrifices (Rom. 12:1) in order that the life of Christ might form within them and bring the transformation. He reminded the Corinthians that as Christ formed in them they became the very temple of his Spirit (1 Cor. 3:16, 6:19). All of this is why, for Paul, to live a gospel-centered life meant, "I have been crucified with Christ and I no longer live, but Christ lives in me. The life I live in the body, I live by faith in the Son of God, who loved me and gave himself for me" (Gal. 2:20).

It is the life of Christ formed in us by the fullness of the Holy Spirit that enables sanctification, effective mission and fruit to the glory of God. Those who only walk in friendship with Jesus can never bear organic fruit of the Spirit, become like Christ or effectively carry out the mission of the Church. Many Christians try to manufacture fruit by teamwork with their friend Jesus. But humans can only produce plastic fruit, which may look nice but will never nourish or impart life. Too many believe their sanctification is up to them, so after "accepting Jesus" they roll up their sleeves in an attempt to become godly through moralistic behavior while ignoring the ongoing power of the gospel—

"Christ in you, the hope of glory." Others hang on to their life agenda but procure Jesus as their "co-pilot" (Really!) to assist them in their ambitions. Friendship theology does not result in Christlikeness or effective mission, nor does it accentuate the power of the gospel to transform lives.

The most helpful word for me to describe the believer's role in sanctification and mission is "cooperation." I don't mean cooperation as in teamwork, but fully cooperating with another's initiative, purpose, agenda and mission. By cooperation I do not mean, *I do my part; God does His,* but rather, I cooperate with God forming the life of Christ in me. Such a spirit of cooperation will embrace without resentment the ways in which the Spirit works within, even if those ways are unpleasant or painful. My part is best expressed by Paul in Ephesians 5:18b, "Be filled with the Spirit." As we feed on Jesus (John 6), by intentionally and continually receiving the sap of the vine, his life is formed and shaped within us so that we become less and Jesus becomes more within us. Cooperation is allowing spiritual digestion of the life of Christ to take place within me. Just as eating stimulates gastrointestinal digestion without my intentionality, so spiritual digestion forms Christ in me when I consume Jesus broken and poured out. Physically, all I have to do is feed, and digestion will work its wonder of giving and strengthening life. Spiritually, all I have to do is feed on Jesus and the Spirit will do his wonder of forming and strengthening the life of Christ within me.

Church, we need to feed on Jesus. Walk with him, talk with him, but feed on him as well. The one who feeds on him will live because of him. Unless you feed on him, you have no life in you. Whoever feeds on him, remains in him and he in you. Consume Christ. Drink in his Spirit. Stay spiritually hungry. Feed as often as you eat; be filled as often as you drink. If I were as hungry spiritually as I am physically, I'd never miss a meal. Feed on Jesus.

The relational principles we learned from David's psalms (ponder, pour out, petition and praise), are instructive and exemplary for feeding on Jesus. The same principles David applied to nurture his life with Adonai can get us started feeding on Jesus. When we follow David's example with a focus of pondering the gospel of Jesus and the object of our petition the

Spirit of Jesus, the life of Christ will form within us. The four "P's" are how David expressed his belief, how he consumed Christ. Remember, every page of scripture is about Jesus—it all points to him. When we feed on Jesus through pondering the gospel, pouring out our hearts, petitioning in the Spirit and praising, the life of Christ takes shape within us to the glory of God.

In Chapter 3 we'll consider how David pondered God as an example for our feeding. Consuming Christ is not just about pondering God but pondering what God has accomplished in the gospel. Nourishing the soul with gospel truth is the starting point for consuming Christ. As you move through the next chapter, prepare to lay down the book, stop reading and ponder the gospel of Jesus. Think deeply about Jesus broken and poured out for your life and satisfaction.

QUESTIONS FOR THOUGHT AND INTERACTION
Chapter 2

1. How is the Old Testament King David an instructive example to your feeding on Jesus?

2. Describe how David engaged his whole heart (mind, will, emotions) with God. Give an example from one of his psalms.

3. How does Psalm 110 illustrate David's intimacy with Jesus Christ?

4. With which of the 4 "P's" do you most identify and why? Which is most obscure or unfamiliar to you and why?

5. How does the opportunity of the Holy Spirit indwelling you (an opportunity David did not have) make you feel?

6. What is even greater than friendship with Jesus? Why?

Chapter 3
Ponder the Gospel

"For my flesh is real food"
(John 6:55)

Although David's example of intimacy with the Lord is insufficient for consuming Christ, it nonetheless provides a helpful starting point. To love someone is to think about them, often. To follow another's example and emulate his life requires intentional observation and thoughtful contemplation of that person's life. God wants believers in Jesus to be like Jesus, and changing one's way of thinking is necessary for that transformation (Rom. 12:2). Changed thinking is the beginning of repentance, the life-changing, ongoing response to the gospel. David's example of intentionally thinking differently about himself, God, life and circumstances by pondering the good news of God is invaluable. It is a starting point for consuming Christ.

To ponder is to think deeply about something. Thinking deeply about the consuming Christ metaphor Jesus gave us in John 6, with repentance as the starting point, leads to feeding as believing. Pondering God, self, life and circumstances through the lens of the gospel is a staple of feeding on Jesus. Intentionally feeding on Jesus is like eating a meal. Hunger draws us to the table, where we intentionally stop other behavior in order to feed. Most meals include meat, the centerpiece of the menu around which sides, appetizers and desserts are selected. In John 6 Jesus taught that the meat of the gospel is himself.

Digested meat creates strength, energy and muscle. It is full of protein and contains all the essential amino acids required by the body for optimum growth of lean, calorie-burning tissue—muscle! Meat is the mainstay of a good meal. Jesus is the meat of a spiritual diet; "My flesh is real food" (John 6:55a). The author of Hebrews said, "Anyone who lives on milk, being still an infant, is not acquainted with the teaching about righteousness. But solid food [MEAT] is for the mature, who by constant use have trained themselves to distinguish good from evil" (Heb. 5:13-14). Since solid food is for the mature, in

Chapter 6 of Hebrews the writer challenges readers to progress beyond elementary teachings about Christ and go on to maturity. In other words, start feeding on the meat of Christ. Hebrews 6:4-6a gives strong warnings to those who would only taste but not consume: "It is impossible for those who have once been enlightened, who have tasted the heavenly gift, who have shared in the Holy Spirit, who have tasted the goodness of the word of God and the powers of the coming age if they fall away, to be brought back to repentance." A tasting of the gospel of Christ won't do; consuming Christ as one eats meat is required. Jesus, broken and poured out, must be digested for transformation to occur, and more than any other food, meat has to be chewed in order to gain the full nutritional value. Spiritually ingesting Jesus, as the body digests meat, becomes life, strength, energy and lean, spiritual muscle.

Isaiah 55:2b-3a, written long before Jesus' incarnation, challenges us to find spiritual nourishment in the right places, "Listen, listen to me, and eat what is good, and your soul will delight in the richest of fare. Give ear and come to me; hear me, that your soul may live." What is the "richest of fare" in this passage? What is the meat that is the soul's delight? It is Jesus! Come to ME (verse 3) and your soul will be nourished, satisfied and full of life. Isaiah 55:2a says, "Why spend money on what is not bread, and your labor on what does not satisfy?" Why waste time and energy on foods that are only spiritual appetizers, salads or side dishes when you can have the main course? The main course to which Isaiah 55 points is Jesus. Be filled with Jesus; he is meat that energizes the soul. A steady diet of Jesus keeps the soul healthy, lean and strong.

David's Satisfaction

David, a strong military man, knew the folly of finding strength in anything but the Lord. "Some trust in chariots and some in horses, but we trust in the name of the LORD our God" (Ps. 20:7). David knew military might was not the nourishment his soul most needed. David's soul longed for something deeper than military or political success— he longed for God.

David's son, Solomon, wrote about the foolishness of seeking nourishment for the soul from wealth. "Do not wear yourself out to get rich; have the wisdom to show restraint. Cast but a glance at riches, and they are gone, for they will surely sprout wings and fly off to the sky like an eagle" (Prov. 23:4-5). Riches and what they can buy satisfy for a moment, but ultimately wealth, like everything other than God, is insufficient to satisfy the soul. Money and possessions are like junk food that tastes good in the short term but provides no substantial nutrients.

Not even human relationships can satisfy the soul, as David no doubt learned through his encounter with Bathsheba when he should have been with his troops. David lost focus from the roof of his palace. He sought to find satisfaction in someone other than the Lord. A familial mess resulted, from which David never recovered. We seek soul satisfaction through relationships when we depend upon and even demand that spouses, children, parents, employers and friends fill our hungry souls, but God did not design human beings with the capacity to satisfy each other's deepest longings. Satisfaction from others may last for a season but eventually all people, even those we love the most, will disappoint us.

Throughout the psalms, David speaks about his soul being satisfied with God. When David felt weary, he went to God's word for satisfaction: "The law is perfect, reviving the soul" (Ps. 19:7a). David is feeding on God's word, compelling him to say, "My soul will be satisfied as with the richest of foods" (Ps. 63:5a) - a proclamation of a satisfied soul. David experienced what Moses taught in Deuteronomy 8:3 and what Jesus declared to Satan in a desperate time of hunger, "Man does not live on bread alone, but on every word that comes from the mouth of God" (Matt. 4:4).

David's satisfaction in God and his enthusiasm for God's word is inspiring, but many people read God's word without experiencing the nourishment and satisfaction of which David spoke. Few people I know, even astute biblical scholars, speak about their souls being satisfied in God as David did. Why not? C.S. Lewis once said, "A man can't be always defending the truth; there must be a time to feed on it" (*Reflections on the Psalms* 95). Did David "feed" on God's word differently than we do? Is there something we can learn, not so much from David's spiritual diet, but from how he consumed God's word? David showed us how he fed on God's word when he wrote Psalms.

Discover Jesus in the Word

For most, reading the Bible is a cognitive exercise where observations are made and information is categorized, because we read to learn something, to gain knowledge. But the purpose of God's word is not just to inform our minds but to feed our souls and ultimately transform our lives with the life and gospel of Jesus. The Bible is primarily revelation, not just information about Jesus. John Calvin wrote, "The scriptures should be read with the aim of finding Christ in them. Whoever turns aside from this object, even though he wears himself out all his life in learning, he will never reach the knowledge of the truth" (Calvin 139). The Bible contains trustworthy theology and historically accurate information, but that is not its primary purpose. The Bible is primarily revelation of Jesus, the Christ who can transform believers into living expressions of his life.

David thought often about God with his mind, but his psalms demonstrate that he also pondered or thought deeply about God affectively. David writes some great theology in Psalm 27 "The Lord is my light and my salvation," but in verse 8 he says, "My heart says of you, 'Seek his face!' Your face, LORD, I will seek." David's soul was not satisfied by theology but by affective engagement with the reality of God. The word "heart" is used over one hundred times in the psalms, evidence of affective engagement with God. God's truth was transformational to David because it affected his heart. As digested food nourishes and transforms the body, so David's pondering God, not just information about God, nourished his soul. The *affective* (arising from feelings or emotion) is where the life of Christ begins to form, in the heart, not just the mind. David expressed his thoughts about God in connection with the emotions, desires and longings of his soul. When David thought of God his emotions were involved, an expression of David's passionate heart for God.

Through affective engagement with God's word, we can grow in the same passion for Jesus that David had. Pondering the gospel, to which all scripture points, feeds the soul because the "meat" of the gospel is Jesus. Affective pondering helps us apprehend the very essence of Jesus. Jonathan Edwards referred to this affective impact as a "due apprehension" (Sproul 54). Edwards' "due apprehension" is more than a cognitive or intellectual understanding. Rather, it is affective, impacting the emotions and passions of the soul. When we gain this due apprehension, we gain God, finding him formed in our very souls.

R.C. Sproul helps us understand this due apprehension by commenting on the essence of Jonathan Edwards' teaching, "We can understand the doctrine with our mind. We may even have a perfectly orthodox understanding of the truth without that truth ever piercing our soul. It is the soul-piercing understanding that we are after, the understanding wrought within us by the Holy Spirit." (Sproul 54) Reading the Bible is a great thing, but if we read it only as an intellectual, cognitive exercise, the true essence of Jesus may never get to our hearts. R. C. Sproul continues, "Knowing that such study [of God's word] is necessary and cannot be circumvented, we are also aware that it is not enough. It may get the word into our minds, but we want more; we want it in our hearts" (Sproul 65). That twelve inch journey from head to heart is one of the toughest terrains the word of God has to travel. God's word penetrated David's heart and his psalms help us see how affectively pondering God feeds the soul. Whether David was being threatened, feeling despair, rejoicing in the good life, running for his life or feeling guilty about his sin, his affective pondering of God fed his soul like meat feeds the body. David was enthralled with God. His soul was captivated by God.

Pondering is a kind of mental and affective rumination. "Rumination" is the word used to describe the digestive process of cattle and other animals who chew cud. These ruminants have stomachs with four chambers. The cud is regurgitation that comes up from one stomach chamber and is further broken down as the animal chews it before swallowing it into another chamber of the stomach. Pondering Jesus is a kind of soul rumination, locking onto a thought of Jesus' essence, character or deeds and then "chewing on it" mentally and affectively. This process brings "nutrients" from the gospel of Jesus to nourish the soul.

The soul or heart also includes the will, so if we hope to

nourish the entire soul with Jesus, truths of Jesus must be ingested into the will. Consuming Christ is not just intellectual and affective but volitional as well. To feed the will with Jesus is to allow the truth of the gospel to impact, influence, change, direct and compel not only big decisions, but common daily decisions. Pondering Jesus, as compelled by the word, transforms the will so that decisions of the soul are different, consistent with the essence, character and commands of Jesus as his life forms within the heart. "If we are to be Christians whose hearts beat and break with the rhythm of the heart of God, we must take on his Word wholeheartedly. . . It means understanding Scripture in its historic, classical context. It means accepting Christ as our Savior and allowing his rule to permeate our thoughts, decisions and actions" (Colson 150).

Affectively and willfully pondering the gospel consistent with the whole of scripture allows the essence, character and decisions of Jesus to be ingested into the thoughts, emotions and will so that the entire being is affected. Add dependence on illumination of the Spirit, and pondering scripture approaches what ancient readers called "lectio divina" or spiritual reading. The term "spiritual reading" sounds mystical but is in reality affectively and volitionally pondering God under the compulsion, guidance and illumination of the Holy Spirit.

Eugene Peterson describes spiritual reading in his excellent work, *Eat This Book*, "This kind of reading named by our ancestors as lectio divina, often translated "spiritual reading," reading that enters our souls as food enters our stomachs, spreads through our blood, and becomes holiness and love and wisdom" (Peterson 4). Spiritual reading changes and nourishes the reader just as a good meal nourishes the body of the eater. "Words spoken or written to us under the metaphor of eating, words to be freely taken in, tasted, chewed, savored, swallowed, and digested, have a very different effect on us from those that come at us from the outside, whether in the form of propaganda or information" (Peterson 10).

The role of the Holy Spirit, who inspired the scripture, is critical in this kind of reading because the Spirit of Jesus works to illumine the soul of the believing reader. "It is difficult to over-estimate the importance of this illumination. Without it the Bible is a closed book practically, with little to charm the reader, because of his inability to grasp its meaning; with it the pages of scripture become luminous, and its beauties grow upon us as, with wonder we explore its exhaustless treasures" (Ridout 190). "This is of what spiritual illumination consists. It is not a mere informing of the mind, or communication of intellectual knowledge, but an experiential and efficacious consciousness of the reality and nature of divine and spiritual things" (Pink 63). Reading and study of the Bible can get the truth of God into our minds, but that doesn't nourish the soul. We must depend on the Holy Spirit to illumine the word as we affectively and volitionally ponder truths of the gospel. Jesus said, "The Spirit gives life; the flesh counts for nothing. The words I have spoken to you are spirit and they are life" (John 6:63). Without the illumination of the Holy Spirit we will not be spiritually nourished, because only the work of the Spirit forms the life of Christ in the soul. The efforts of the flesh count for nothing—they have no nutritional value for the soul.

Pondering Jesus is delightful, like savoring a quality meal. "How amazing are the deeds of the Lord! All who delight in him should ponder them" (Ps. 111:2). When we ponder Jesus our emotions will be renewed. "My soul will be satisfied as with the richest of food; with singing lips my mouth will praise you" (Ps. 63:5). David's soul was nourished and given peace by the Lord even when things were chaotic around him: "You have made known to me the path of life; you will fill me with joy in your presence, with eternal pleasures at your right hand" (Ps. 16:11). C.S. Lewis said, "God designed the human machine to run on Himself. He Himself is the fuel our spirits were designed to burn, or the food our spirits were designed to feed on. There isn't any other. God can't give us happiness and peace apart from Himself" (*Mere Christianity* 54). When we ponder Jesus, involving the mind, will, and emotions under the illumination of the Holy Spirit, God nourishes us. Unless the Spirit of Jesus fills, captures and affectively enthralls our souls we will be malnourished.

Ingest Jesus Affectively and Willfully: Ponder Gospel

Since all of scripture reveals Christ, we can follow David's example of pondering to feed on Jesus. Read Psalm 103 a verse at a time and then, from the content of each verse, finish the phrase *"Jesus, you are the one who . . . ."* For example, verse one says, "Praise His holy name," so "Jesus, you are the one who is holy." I've been trying to intellectually explain the holiness of God for decades and I can't do it adequately. But I've pondered God's holiness in my heart long enough to apprehend a measure of his holiness, even though I cannot adequately explain that aspect of his being. The holiness of Christ nourishes the soul. Gaining an affective sense of the holiness of Jesus Christ can be life-changing. Expressions of God's holiness in Revelation 4, Ezekiel 1 and Isaiah 6 inspire complete awe and satisfaction in knowing, really apprehending Jesus. It is not necessary to fully explain Jesus' holiness intellectually before the soul can be enthralled, satisfied, and fed by the life of Jesus.

Pondering Psalm 103:3, "God you are the one who . . . forgives all my sins," applies the work of Christ on the cross to the heart for forgiveness of sin. Feeding on that simple little phrase in the morning rejuvenates the soul to start a new day no matter how many poor choices, failures or sins were committed the day before. Continued rumination reminds the soul of this profound truth and empowers forgiveness.

Continued pondering of Psalm 103:14, "God you are the one who . . . knows how I am formed," reminds the heart that Jesus, whose life is forming in the believer, knows the depths of the soul, our very DNA. Think back to a time when you tried to explain what you were feeling and thinking to another person, who nodded in affirmation but didn't seem to affectively apprehend—they just didn't get it. God knows how we are formed. The incarnate Jesus not only understands but empathizes with the heart of the believer. The Lord Jesus Christ knows and has experienced the thoughts, intentions, desires and longings of the human heart. The gospel incarnate feeds the soul with confidence.

David wrote Psalm 13 under duress, expressing emotions of loneliness, abandonment, rejection, confusion, defeat and despair:

How long, O LORD? Will you forget me

forever? How long will you hide your face from me? How long must I wrestle with my thoughts and every day have sorrow in my heart? How long will my enemy triumph over me? Look on me and answer, O LORD my God. Give light to my eyes, or I will sleep in death; my enemy will say, 'I have overcome him,' and my foes will rejoice when I fall. (Ps. 13:1-4)

But notice what happens after four verses of pouring out the negative in his soul. In verse 5, David intentionally refocuses on God's love and salvation and, when he does, the whole tone of what he is expressing changes. "But I trust in your unfailing love; my heart rejoices in your salvation" (Ps. 13:5). The affective side of David's soul turned in an almost schizophrenic way from defeat and despair to joyful confidence, expressed in 13:6 as "I will sing to the LORD; for he has been good to me." Because David affectively pondered God's unfailing love, his soul was nourished, enriched, encouraged and satisfied in God.

Psalm 13 demonstrates the transformational power of pondering the gospel. This transformation is evident in many psalms as the soul of the psalmist progresses through deep despair and lament into wonder, joy and peace of the gospel. Matthew Jacoby in his analysis of the psalms says, "In the lament psalms, even in the most seemingly despairing ones, the psalmists deliberately bring two things into tension. They deliberately highlight the reality of their situation as it stands in tension with the reality of God and his promises. As both realities are amplified, this very tension then becomes the seedbed for faith and hope. Faith is conceived by the injection of the divine promise into the open wound of a heart that has allowed itself to be wounded by reality" (Jacoby 86). This is how the truth of Christ transforms the soul that ponders the gospel.

Thoughts of Jesus' essence, character and deeds can be compelled from pondering most texts of scripture. Anticipating what a text reveals about Jesus is the beginning point of pondering gospel. Most of us can remember first learning to read and not remembering what we read. It still happens to me sometimes. I can read an entire page and turn to the next without having any idea what I just read. This kind of "attention deficit reading" is often how we read the Bible. We read it because we know we are supposed to, but what we read fails to stick in our minds—let alone penetrate our souls. When reading a passage of scripture, intentionally look for what it reveals about Jesus and the gospel. Then take that "bite" of gospel revelation or thought of Jesus and chew on it (ruminate) as you would a good piece of meat. Savor the thought; ingest all the nutrients from it. Enjoy it and let not only the thought, but the very essence and life, of Jesus be ingested into your soul through God's word.

Two recent examples of my own pondering the gospel as prompted by scriptural revelation may bring encouragement. The first is from an instructional text, James 1:19-20: "My dear brothers, take note of this: Everyone should be quick to listen, slow to speak and slow to become angry, for man's anger does not bring about the righteous life that God desires." This text reveals that God desires me to live a righteous life—an outworking of the gospel. As I thought deeply about Jesus, I remembered that I'm not saved by my righteousness, because even my very best deeds are like filthy rags before God (Isa. 64:6). So any righteousness that will ever exist in me is a gift of Jesus being formed in me. Through more pondering, I realized that man's anger does not bring about righteousness. My anger hinders the formation of the righteousness of Christ in me. That little "bite" of pondering God's passion for the righteousness of his Son to form in me made me more responsive to the instruction in verse 19, 'be quick to listen, slow to speak and slow to become angry." Verse 21 provided fresh motivation to "get rid of all moral filth and the evil that is so prevalent and humbly accept the word planted in you." Pouring out anger and moral filth while being quick to listen and slow to speak helps form the life of Christ in me.

A second example came from a narrative of Easter Sunday morning in John 20:1-18. When Mary Magdalene arrived and looked in the tomb, she saw it was empty and assumed someone had stolen Jesus' body. Mary told Peter and John, who also came and looked in the tomb. Verse 9 says they did not understand what was happening. Then, according to verses 10 and 11, Peter and John went home but Mary stayed outside the tomb crying.

She took a second look and saw two angels. After some dialogue with those angels she turned around and saw Jesus, her third look, but didn't recognize him in the darkness through her tears. Finally, after Jesus spoke her name, Mary turned toward him and recognized him. Mary looked four times before recognizing Jesus' presence, even though he was there the whole time. He wasn't where she expected to find him, but he was there, in the darkness, and from that darkness he called her by name. Pondering Jesus' abiding presence compelled me to persevere in seeking him in dark and desperate circumstances.

Jesus enters our darkness and calls us by name to come to him. Nourishment gained from pondering Jesus as revealed in that beautiful narrative enriched my life and became the sermon I preached on Easter Sunday morning. Mary pushed into the empty darkness by persistently looking for Jesus. Her persistence paid off as she was the first human to see the resurrected Christ. Peter and John failed to persist in seeking Jesus and went back home to normal life.

Before you go back or move on, look for Jesus in the dark places through pondering the gospel revealed in scripture. When life feels empty and dark, press into that darkness and persistently search for Jesus through another look at scripture, with much pondering. Pondering the enduring presence of Christ in the dark, empty times of life feeds the transformational power of the gospel.

My soul was recently nourished through pondering the gospel as revealed in the story of Naomi and Boaz in the Old Testament book of Ruth. Naomi lived in the harsh reality of a broken world, having lost a husband and two sons. Naomi told people to call her Mara, which means "bitter," since her life had been so bitter. She said, "It is more bitter for me than for you, because the Lord's hand has gone out against me! . . . The Lord has afflicted me; the Almighty has brought misfortune upon me" (Ruth 1:13b, 21b). God providentially led Naomi and Ruth (her daughter-in-law) to Boaz, a kinsman redeemer of Naomi's family. Naomi knew what a kinsman redeemer could do for them, and she trusted Boaz with amazing faith (Ruth 2:22, 3:2-6, 18). Boaz married Ruth who later birthed a son named Obed. Naomi held and cared for Obed as she would her own son, considering Obed a gift from the Lord. Obed would later father Jesse, who then fathered the man with a passionate heart for God, King David.

Of Naomi it was said in Ruth 4:14, "Praise be to the Lord, who this day has not left you without a kinsman redeemer." That's gospel! Praise be to God who has not left us without a kinsman redeemer. Jesus, our kinsman redeemer, redeems us from the bitterness of this broken world. My soul was nourished with the life of Christ as I pondered the gospel revealed through Boaz, which fed the formation of the life of Christ through the illumination of scripture by the Holy Spirit.

Pondering Jesus Revealed through Creation

Another venue or plate upon which God serves the gospel to our souls is the creation around us. Just as God's word, God's creation expresses Jesus' heart, essence and character. John 1:3 says, "Through him [Jesus] all things were made; without him nothing was made that has been made." As you can know the artist by observing the painting or the author by his writings, so you can know Jesus by pondering what he created. "What may be known about God is plain to them, because God has made it plain to them. For since the creation of the world God's invisible qualities—his eternal power and divine nature—have been clearly seen, being understood from what has been made, so that men are without excuse" (Rom. 1:19-20).

Years ago I was leading a traditional church through a transition into a more contemporary style of worship. If you've tried that you know it's not much fun. During a brief vacation from it all, I was sitting on the porch of a lake house in a northern Michigan woods pondering why the Lord Jesus had allowed me to get into this situation. I was trying to lead seven hundred worshippers within which there were at least ten sub-group preferences of worship style. We had hymnal huggers, hand raisers, camp chorus clutchers, classical types, arms crossed stoics, put a guitar around your neck and sandals on your feet dudes and dudettes, grind out the electrics loud lovers, "how about letting the drummer lead for once" guys and "the piano always leads" ladies (both of whom offended the chorister, who had always done it that way). Even the choristers fought secretly with the organist for leadership control.

As I sat in the woods, enjoying the glass-like calm surface of the lake before me, a small breeze came up, which blew ripples on the lake and stirred the leaves in the trees. As I pondered, the breeze reminded me of the wind of Jesus' Spirit and I found myself praying that the Spirit would blow strong through my congregation. I thought maybe the Spirit could blow all those music preferences into one and then the "worship wars" would cease. As I pondered, I began to praise Jesus for the variety of trees he created: oak, maple, aspen, poplar, birch and several varieties of pine. I noticed when the wind blew through the trees that each tree responded differently. The oak leaves moved slowly and rather stiffly, whereas the birch and aspen leaves fluttered and danced as if injected with electric current. The pine needles seemed to move the least but made the most noise, a unique whistling. Then it struck me. Those trees responded like the people in the congregation—each one's unique response compelled by the wind of the Spirit of Christ. How lifeless and predictable a woods would be if each tree responded the same way to the wind. How lifeless the congregation of Christ's church would be if each person worshipped the same way.

That insight of Jesus and His people from creation transformed me. It helped me to value each person's preference of worship style and to appreciate musical variety. That moment of pondering Christ changed my leadership and still impacts me today. Pondering or "chewing" on Jesus is transformational, not just informational.

I've grown to love sitting outside and carefully considering what creation reveals to me about my Creator. A few years back I started a "Creation Journal" just to record deep thoughts about God revealed in creation. I add to that journal whenever I experience some fresh gospel insight into the character or essence of Jesus expressed through His creation. Writing down my thoughts helps me to affectively and volitionally ponder Jesus. So whether you are thinking about creation or reading scripture, jot down thoughts of Jesus that come to your mind and ponder them. Feed on those thoughts of Jesus, ruminate on them.

A Method for Pondering God

It may be helpful to have a method or process to follow

when affectively and volitionally pondering Jesus. "Setting the table" of God's word a certain way encourages feeding on Jesus. No matter how the gospel is served up, remember Jesus is meat broken for the soul ("my flesh is real food") and the way to ingest that meat is to chew (ruminate) and savor it. The outcome is the life of Christ formed in the soul, which creates satisfaction. Whether reading scripture or pondering Jesus from some other "plate," like creation, lock your thoughts onto him with intentionality and chew!

For those of you who like steps, here are some to get you started:

1. Come to the table: Pray first—the means by which we gain illumination of the Spirit. (Eph 1:18) Then read a passage of scripture, looking for what it says about the gospel. Look for revelation of Jesus, not just information.

2. Take a bite: When the Spirit reveals something to you about Jesus, stop reading—that's your first bite. Write down specific thoughts about Jesus (essence, character, deeds) that the Holy Spirit reveals to you from that text.

3. Chew on it: Think deeply, affectively and volitionally about how the illumined truth of Christ changes your perspective on today, relationships, work, the future, your feelings, your thinking and your decisions. Write out thoughts and feelings the Spirit compels as you chew on the truth about Jesus.

4. Ruminate: Throughout the day, intentionally bring the truth of Jesus back into conscious and deliberate thought (rumination) while allowing the Spirit to freshly illumine those gospel truths in your soul.

5. Swallow: Hold on to the truths you've pondered; remember them and ruminate often. Each cycle of rumination provides nutrients from the life of Christ. Once meat is swallowed, the nutrients it provides are naturally ingested.

Try an example from Isaiah
1. Come to the table: Pray first for the Spirit to illumine the text

before you. Read Isaiah 43:1-7 looking for what it reveals about Jesus. You should be able to identify at least ten to fifteen ways the Lord relates to people from this passage.

2. Take a bite: Write down the things you notice the text says about the gospel: God is Creator and Redeemer; all things were created through Jesus. God is always with us and Jesus said, "I will never leave you or forsake you." God values people; Jesus suffered the cross for us. God gathers people together; in Christ we are one. God created people with a purpose; we are God's workmanship, created in Christ Jesus to do good works. Now chew on that gospel of Jesus!

3. Chew on it: Think deeply, affectively and volitionally about how these revelations of Jesus change your perspective. How is this thought of Jesus significant for today? Here's a sample list of some "chewing thoughts" from the Isaiah text:

a. God is recreating me as the Spirit forms the life of Christ in me. God gave me talents, personality and skills. I can be satisfied with who I am becoming because God is recreating me in Jesus, who gives me gifts of the Spirit to use for his glory.

b. Jesus is my Redeemer. Even when I sin, I'm forgiven and Jesus brings me back. Today is a new start because Jesus redeems every day. I made mistakes yesterday, but today I have another chance to use the talents and skills the Lord Jesus has entrusted to my care because I'm forgiven.

c. Jesus is with me, so I have a better chance of success. Whether I use my skills well today or not, Jesus is still with me and will never forsake me. He will redeem my failures and motivate me to use the skills and abilities he's forming in me.

d. Jesus values me; the cross is my eternal reminder. Jesus redeems me and stays with me because he values me. The Creator Lord of the universe values me and wants to be with me—all the time. I know I am precious to Jesus because he gave his life, broken and poured out, to form his life in me. I am crucified with him so that his life might be formed in me.

e. Jesus gathers people together. He is working to mend strained, distant relationships in my life. Jesus is working to bring me together with difficult people and will empower and help me as I pursue gospel-centered restoration when there is tension or conflict. When I feel distance from my wife or children, Jesus will empower me to initiate gospel reconciliation without stubbornness. Jesus is not pleased when I have conflict with someone at work, so I'll keep striving to get on the same page with that person.

f. I'm being recreated in Christ to glorify him. I have a reason to live, work and play that is bigger than myself. Jesus' mission empowers me to see interpersonal interactions as missional opportunities.

In summary, Jesus, who is forming his life in me, has redeemed me, he stays with me always, values and delights in me, is working to restore all the strained relationships in my life and has given me the privilege to live for his glory. Imagine starting each day with this kind of nourishing spiritual breakfast!

4. Ruminate: Intentionally repeat the process of affectively and volitionally thinking about the same gospel truths throughout the day. A wise Bible professor once gave his students an assignment to read a verse and return the next class period with three written applications of that verse. The assignment the next day was to write five more applications of the same verse. The following day's assignment was to write ten applications of the same text, and on it continued for several class periods. The professor was teaching his students to chew on the gospel in order to digest every morsel it reveals about Jesus. As you ruminate on gospel truths about Jesus revealed in scripture, your soul will be nourished by the life of Christ in you.

5. Swallow: Ingest gospel truths of Jesus into the soul by holding those truths in your heart all day long. Eating is one thing, digestion is another. As long as the food stays in the digestive system nutrients are gained from it. As long as gospel truths that reveal Jesus consciously stay in the soul, spiritual nutrients that give strength, energy, power and perseverance will be ingested to the formation of the life of Christ.

Try an example on your own:
  1. Come to the table: Pray for spiritual illumination and

then read Psalm 65.

2. **Take a bite:** Write down gospel thoughts about Jesus that Psalm 65 reveals.

3. **Chew on it:** Write out affective and volitional thoughts of how the gospel of Jesus changes your perspective.

4. **Ruminate:** Think again about these gospel truths and then write how they impact life and faith.

5. **Swallow:** Lock on to gospel thoughts of Jesus and ingest the spiritual nutrition they give.

Now ponder a New Testament narrative, Mark 8:27-30.
1. **Come to the table:** Pray for spiritual illumination and then read Mark 8:27-30.

2. **Take a bite:** List gospel truths about Jesus that Mark 8:27-30 reveals:
   a. Jesus spent time with his disciples in several places.
   b. Jesus asked the disciples who others thought he was.
   c. Jesus wanted to know who his disciples thought he was.
   d. Jesus was concerned about others knowing his true identity at that time

3. **Chew on it:** Jesus loved to be with people. Jesus had concerns about timing and how others might respond to him since he didn't want anyone else to know who he was right then.

4. **Ruminate:** Jesus went multiple places with his disciples. He is with me at work, at the ball game, while traveling and even in the dark places. Timing is important. Jesus' timing is perfect so I should trust his timing over my impulsive nature.

5. **Swallow:** Ingest the spiritual nutrients from these gospel truths about Jesus. I wonder what people think of me: Do they think of Jesus when they encounter me? If the life of Jesus is being formed in my soul I shouldn't feel insecure about what others think of me. I should pray, asking Jesus to reveal his life through me. When I do that, I'll receive even more spiritual nutrition.

All scripture reveals the gospel of Jesus Christ. Read spiritually; chew on scripture to intentionally feed your soul. Read looking for what a particular story or passage in the Bible reveals about Jesus. Those gospel truths will nourish your soul. A regular diet of pondering gospel will feed your soul and develop strong, lean spiritual muscle. The strength of the life of Christ forming in you will enable you to face challenges and problems with a new sense of confidence and optimism. Feed on Jesus as consistently as you feed your body. Ponder the life of Christ, broken and poured out for you.

In Chapter 4, we'll consider one of the great invitations of God in scripture—pouring out the soul. This invitation, encouraged on more than one occasion, has largely been ignored in preaching, writing and practice in the American Church. This is tragic, because pouring out one's soul is a primary expression of trust, as Psalm 62:8 makes clear. Pouring out the soul is illustrated in nearly every psalm David wrote. Pouring out the soul is sometimes painful and always messy, but is a delightful necessity for fully feeding on Jesus. So prepare to think through a repulsive metaphor and read on.

QUESTIONS FOR THOUGHT AND INTERACTION
Chapter 3

1. Chewing is both instinctive and intentional. Describe how pondering God is both.

2. Once we've chewed and swallowed some meat, ingestion of nutrients happens automatically. How does this happen spiritually when we ponder God?

3. Watching someone else eat doesn't nourish, but it may encourage me to eat. How do others encourage or discourage your feeding on Jesus?

4. A Sunday sermon can be like a good steak for the soul, but by Tuesday it no longer provides nourishment unless. . . What?

5. How does pondering God (different from just gaining knowledge) affect the mind, will and emotions?

6. In what ways do we try to "take a bite of God" without taking the time to chew, ponder and digest?

7. Once you've tasted and seen that the Lord is good, what will you do next? How can you keep that "good taste" in your soul?

Chapter 4
Pour Out Your Heart

"Pour out your hearts like water to the Lord"
(Lamentations 2:19 NLT)

Some years ago I was traveling with my family and we stopped for a late evening snack at a fast food restaurant which was offering a limited time meatloaf sandwich. I'm not a big meatloaf guy, (meat served in loaf form seems wrong to me), but the promotional picture on the menu above the counter enticed me. So I ordered one with lots of onions and "special" sauce. I ate it with gusto because it was quite good.

Two hours later something started going on in my normally impenetrable "cast iron stomach." At first the discomfort felt like something that would pass without major incident, but as the pain intensified I began to realize this was going to require a stop. Soon the cramping and nausea became extreme and it was then I realized how this was going to end. This was headed for regressive digestive crisis.

I did all I could to avoid what I knew was coming. I practiced the best breathing techniques I could remember from the days of childbirth classes with my wife. I tried sitting very still and focusing on a distant point. I tried moving around and stretching my legs. I opened the window and cranked the air conditioner on full, but the dreaded event seemed more imminent. Finally, I succumbed to the inevitable and pulled over at an interstate service plaza in order to spare my family.

I was able to make it all the way into the restroom, which I soon realized was no real advantage. A restroom in a high traffic, public place like an interstate service plaza at 2:30 in the morning, is disgusting from the kneeling vantage point, but it didn't really matter, because what was about to happen was much more urgent. One rest stop wasn't enough to purge me completely of the "bad meatloaf," and I found the next two stops to be no cleaner or more inviting than the first. What a horrible memory! I promised God I would never eat a limited time, fast food meatloaf sandwich again, and I've kept my promise.

This unusual function of the digestive system is repulsive; we don't even like thinking about it. According to an online study of thirty traditionally bad sounds, the sound of vomiting is the worst sound in the world, but this nasty digestive disturbance is sometimes necessary and is an instructive part of Jesus' feeding metaphor that helps us understand spiritual nourishment.

I hope you are tracking with the metaphor and are thinking about all the "bad meatloaf" we ingest into our souls. Some "meatloaf" is there because we foolishly craved it, like pornography, the power to control others, inappropriate relationships or the coveting of things. Other "bad meatloaf" is in the soul against our will, like fear and discouragement, and some because of our choices—guilt, pride, self-centeredness and impurity. "Relational toxins" cause us to feel envy, loneliness, pain, frustration and conflict.

How "bad meatloaf" gets in our souls is less the point than the fact that it is there. It is a toxin God never intended to be part of spiritual digestion. The toxin in our souls is inescapable because we were born into a broken world and are, ourselves, broken and poisoned by sin to the core of our being (Eph. 2:1-3). We are totally depraved.

This innate brokenness leads us to crave "bad meatloaf" in the first place. Back to my fast food experience, "What was I thinking?" Common sense says a limited time meatloaf sandwich from a fast food restaurant is not a healthy choice. I should have been smarter. I put something into my stomach because it appealed to my desires even though it had a high risk of making me sick. I saw it. I bought it. I ate it. I puked it!

My son and his wife had a Cocker Spaniel mix puppy. The puppy, who apparently had yet to fully develop cognitively, ate grass, sticks and whatever he could scrounge from the burn pile. He chewed on stones from the driveway and ate other things too disgusting to mention. That puppy was as happy as he could be eating whatever his snout led him to, but he had no understanding that the bad things he ingested would soon be rejected—which happened almost every night.

Think about how much we are like that young puppy. Whatever appeals to our sense of desire, we ingest. If it is for sale we buy it, we take it and we "eat" it. It soon turns sour to us, like a limited time fast food meatloaf sandwich. We pursue things without price tags, like a "love fix," whether by genuine love or by a temporary fulfillment of lust. The person desperate for love rarely gives thought to whether the object of his satisfaction is "bad meatloaf" or a steak full of protein. Only later is the "meatloaf" recognized for what it was. Once it turns sour in the soul, only one thing will stop nauseous progression—get rid of it.

But just like physical nausea, we are averse to soul vomit, even though God invites us to pour out our souls. Some may hate pouring out the soul even more than pouring out the stomach. Physical nausea, though common to everyone, involves a degree of shame, especially if you can't make it to an interstate service plaza in time. But with pouring out the soul, shame is the core of the issue. Shame keeps us from pouring out the contents of our souls leaving us with a consistent, dull, spiritual nausea. Shame comes from an instinctive knowledge that what is in our souls innately and by our choices deeply disappoints and offends our Creator. So we hide our souls from God just as the first humans hid themselves in the Garden of Eden after they sinned. We cover our shame to avoid disclosing it. Shame is a toxin that holds the soul in a painful, sick, nauseous, cramped spiritual existence.

God has given us a means to purge our souls of bad meat; the Bible calls it pouring out the heart. But for some reason, perhaps the messy, shameful aspect of it, pouring out the heart is an invitation in scripture that many fail to accept or even know about. Pouring out the heart, if you allow the metaphor of the physical counterpart to instruct your mind, leads to peace in the soul. But we hate to do it. Just as we go to extremes to avoid digestive vomiting, so we try to avoid spiritual vomiting, even though pouring out the soul it is one of the great gifts of God to his people.

Confession is one aspect of pouring out the soul. Confession by definition means agreement. Soul confession is a spirit of agreement with God about the bad meat we allow in our souls, whether it's our sin nature, someone else's sin against us or the sinful brokenness of the world. Confession can be expressed to others or to God alone, but either way—it gets the poison out.

Many people perceive confession negatively because of imprinting from past religious experiences. If that describes you, stop and pray; ask God to fill you with a fresh and right understanding of confession. Confession is a good thing. John wrote in his first letter, "If we confess our sins, he is faithful and just to forgive our sins and to cleanse us from all unrighteousness" (1 John 1:9). Did you catch the "cleanse" part? That's the result of pouring out, cleansing! David said in Psalm 38:18a, "I confess my iniquity." Why? "Because I am troubled by my sin." Confess sin; pour it out, because it troubles the soul. Sin creates nausea in the heart; pour it out!

Many Christians think of confession as a thing they did when they first trusted in Christ, but confession is part of an ongoing response to the gospel. Christians are not people who've stopped sinning, but people who never stop confessing their sin and repenting of it in Christ. Expectations of people or God can be subtly sinful and should be regularly poured out. Anger, which managed improperly causes many sins, is a result of unmet or disappointed expectations. Ask the Spirit to point out inappropriate expectations of your heart so you can pour those out to Jesus. Expectations quickly morph into covetousness, so let go of them by pouring them out. Pouring out of expectations, self-centeredness, entitlements, pride and other subtleties of the heart should be a regular part of gospel-centered Christian living.

But pouring out the heart is broader than confession of sin. I have a friend who struggles with drug addiction and went through a painful divorce some years back. During that time he learned the skill of pouring out his soul to Jesus. Prior to his second divorce, my friend lost a close brother and a precious five-year-old daughter to death. He experienced immense pain in his soul. I could not take the pain from him but counseled him to pour it out to his loving Savior. When asked how it was going for him, he once replied, "I'm just throwing up on God." He learned the skill of pouring out the pain in his heart before God.

David poured out stress, anxiety, frustration and helplessness before God. He poured out his anger and vented to God about the wicked prospering. He poured out his circumstances, conflicts, troubles, challenges and decisions before God. David's poured-out heart is expressed in the psalms, the most vulnerable and intimate expressions of the soul recorded in scripture.

Pouring out the soul is not just a purging of the negative. There is great value in pouring out both positive and negative emotions, thoughts, choices, desires, questions and circumstances. Both soul and heart refer to the human center of the mind, will and emotions, so to pour out the heart or soul is much more than, "I did or thought something bad so now I have to tell someone about it." Pouring out the soul is releasing or emptying everything that is inside the heart to God. It is how we surrender all to Jesus Christ. Pour it all out. Entrust the depths of your heart to the Lordship of Christ.

Pouring out the heart to Jesus can be a regular, intentional part of my spiritual feeding routine, but pouring out should also be spontaneous. While writing just now, I overhead a person in our office say something that, although not about me, seemed inappropriate; and I found my soul troubled by what I heard. I lost productivity in writing because of my troubled heart. It was not a crisis, just a negative, cynical comment made by one of our staff pastors. I tried to disregard it and move on. But the experience "hooked me" and paralyzed my writing, so I stopped and poured out my heart to God. I took some paper and wrote to God how I felt as best I could articulate. As I poured out my soul, I wondered if my heart needed an attitude adjustment, or if the person who made the comments needed an attitude adjustment, or perhaps both.

After pouring out my thoughts and emotions, I felt a sense of peace, at least enough to start writing again. My soul is still not totally at peace. I'll keep wrestling with this and will probably pour out more tomorrow morning when I have my daily "pour out to Jesus" time. Pouring out the soul is a practical thing that should be a part of our everyday experience.

Why does God want us to pour out our hearts to Him? Is it so God can be informed about what is going on inside of us? Is it because God doesn't want to be in the dark about what we are thinking? Does God fear that we harbor negative feelings against him? Is God concerned that others will know us better than he does or that we'll confide in others before him? Of course not! God is all-knowing, including knowing the human heart: "O LORD; you have searched me and you know me. You know when I sit and when I rise; you perceive my thoughts from afar. You discern my going out and my lying down; you are familiar with all my ways. Before a word is on my tongue you know it completely, O LORD" (Ps. 139:1-4). God doesn't need me to pour out my heart so he can be better informed. God wants me to pour out my soul because he loves me and knows that pouring out my heart to him has value for me. Pouring out is healthy for our hearts and that's why God invites us to do it.

Many Christians are malnourished because they are spiritually nauseous most of the time. A person who feels nauseous is not going to eat, chew or swallow, and long periods of nausea that hinder chewing or swallowing cause spiritual malnutrition. Healthy people who fail to chew and swallow will eventually become unhealthy people. Christians who live with a continual, low grade spiritual nausea caused by guilt, shame, anger or resentment will not thrive because they don't feel like feeding. Psalm 32:3-5 describes the internal discomfort of a soul that needs to be poured out because it is bound up with the nausea of guilt. David described an aching in his bones (Ps 32:3) when he held sin in his heart instead of pouring it out. In verse 5 through the end of the psalm, David expressed the healthy freedom that results when the soul is poured out. Pouring out the soul, although awkward, messy and disgusting at times, is healthy, and that's why God invites us to pour it all out on him.

God's Invitation to Pour Out the Heart
David, who modeled this idea more than any other biblical character, said, "Trust in him [God] at all times, O people; pour out your hearts to him, for God is our refuge" (Ps. 62:8). The parallelism of this verse (one phrase amplifies another) indicates that pouring out the heart (phrase # 2) is an expression of trust (phrase # 1) and trust is the word that best describes ongoing faith in Christ. Psalm 62:8 teaches us how to trust by pouring out our soul to the Lord, who doesn't qualify the invitation: whatever is in there, pour it out. It can be good, bad or indifferent—pour it out. Whether it's sin, something positive, a perplexing scenario or something minor that causes a troubling of the soul, God wants us to pour it out on him as an expression of trust.

Jeremiah was a prophet who continually poured out his heart

to the Lord. Jeremiah lived in the burned and desolate city of Jerusalem after the Babylonians ravaged it in 586 B.C. and deported most of Jerusalem's inhabitants. During that horrible time Jeremiah wrote a book of laments from his soul. Jeremiah's Lamentations are expressions of a poured-out heart. Jeremiah poured out his heart to the Lord and encouraged anyone who was left in the city to do the same, "Arise, cry out in the night, as the watches of the night begin; pour out your heart like water in the presence of the Lord" (Lam. 2:19a). It's graphic and messy but so very important for spiritual health and vitality.

The same principle is communicated in Psalm 55:22, "Cast your cares on the LORD and he will sustain you; he will never let the righteous fall." I'm not much of a fisherman, but I think the best cast is usually the one farthest from you. Notice this "casting" is not a random throwing of something as far as you can in no particular direction. Rather, we are told to cast cares on a personal God. This is an important distinction, because pouring out the heart has become a common psychological technique encouraged by psychologists, therapists and counselors, who recognize the value of offloading stress. Getting it out has value, but pouring out the soul to God is something profoundly different because God is personal and has invited us to cast our cares upon him. Psychological venting is random and can hurt other people. It can be quite counterproductive in family and work relationships. But pouring out the heart to God is a profoundly different experience because God has come to us in a profoundly personal way—the gospel of the Lord Jesus. In the New Testament Peter said, "Cast all your anxiety on him because he cares for you" (1 Pet. 5:7). Pouring out the heart to Jesus is trusting someone who cares deeply about you, a Personal Being who takes delight in you. Pouring out the soul is more than offloading stress, it is trusting a personal, caring, loving Savior with the stress of your soul. Jesus is not only big enough to take your stress and keep it from coming back on you, but he can also redeem that stress into something positive (Rom. 8:28).

My wife and I are dear friends with a woman who experienced the betrayal of divorce. During the divorce, and for months after, our friend often called to pour out her feelings of pain, abandonment and betrayal. We gladly listened and invited her to pour out her heart to us any time she needed. One night her call woke us around 3:30 a.m. She explained it had been a hard night and she'd been unable to sleep. She said she needed to pour out her soul to us. I'll never forget what she said: "I know you are both barely awake, but it's okay. Just lay the phone down on the bed between you and let me talk. I don't care if you fall back asleep; I just need to talk knowing you guys are on the other end of the phone." It wasn't enough for our friend to randomly throw off her feelings; she needed to pour them out to a person who loved her deeply. She needed to know she was trusting the depths of her broken soul to people who deeply cared for her. God loves us deeply and responds to the poured-out heart with listening, empathy, love, tenderness, encouragement, comfort, courage and strength. A human counselor can listen and receive what we pour out, but only God can directly inject into the soul what is needed when the heart is poured out - the life of Christ.

The invitation to pour out the soul is affirmed by Paul in the New Testament: "Do not be anxious about anything, but in everything by prayer and petition with thanksgiving present your requests to God" (Phil. 4:6). If your soul is anxious, pour it out to God in prayer. Do this regardless of the source of anxiety or trouble: "Do not be anxious about anything" and, "in everything by prayer and petition. . . ." This invitation is for anytime, any context, any stress, anybody. If Philippians 4:6 is read in isolation from its context, one might expect what God gives in response to a poured-out heart is a change of circumstances. We'd like the next verse to say, "And God, who really loves you, will go to bat for you and fix the situation. God, who loves you even more than your grandmother, will change people's opinions and manipulate the situation so it is more tolerable for you." But pouring out the soul does not mean God will get us out of a mess we helped create. God can do the impossible and sometimes, when we pray to him, we hope he'll wave his "God-wand" and do magical things in our circumstances.

In times of stress and anxiety it is easy to forget what God most wants for us—to form the life of Christ in us. When we pour out our souls, we position ourselves to receive the life of Christ. If God were to wave his "God-wand" and "fix" our situations, we'd say thanks and move on. There would be a brief moment of gratitude but no desire or commitment for the life of Christ to be formed in us through trials. If, instead, God listens, empathizes and cares without "fixing anything" we'll share even more of our souls with him. When we do, the Spirit pours more and more of the life of Christ into us. God delights in us when we pour out our hearts to him because in doing so, we open our souls to receive the life of Christ.

Forming Christ within is about character development, and Christ-like character is developed most through "cross-like" circumstances. Gold is refined through heat and pressure as Peter reminds us: ". . . for a little while you may have had to suffer grief in all kinds of trials. These have come so that your faith—of greater worth than gold, which perishes even though refined by fire—may be proved genuine and may result in praise, glory and honor when Jesus Christ is revealed" (1 Pet. 1:6-7). The trials of life refine us and mature us. Circumstances stretch us and develop our character, fashioning us more and more into the glorious image of Jesus Christ. E.M. Bounds reminds us that trouble is God's servant:

> Trouble is under the control of Almighty God, and is one of his most efficient agents in fulfilling his purposes and in perfecting his saints. God's hand is in every trouble which breaks into the lives of men. Not that he directly and arbitrarily orders every unpleasant experience of life. Not that he is personally responsible for every painful and afflicting thing which comes into the lives of his people. But no trouble is ever turned loose in this world and comes into the life of saint or sinner, but comes with divine permission, and is allowed to exist and do its painful work with God's hand in it or on it, carrying out his gracious designs of redemption. (Bounds 49)

God redeems trouble by forming Christ within - it's the way of the gospel.

Trouble leads to transformation and calamity leads to Christlikeness. Pain develops perseverance and desperation demands dependence. The Spirit will form the life of Christ in

73

believers through circumstances as they trust him and cooperate with him.

Whether God "fixes" things according to our expectation or not, he promises to place something in us that transcends difficult circumstances—the life of Christ. And where Christ is, there is peace. God replaces the stress we pour out with a wonderful blessing - soul peace. This is the promise of Philippians 4:7, "And the peace of God, which transcends all understanding, will guard your hearts and your minds in Christ Jesus." There is no promise of changed circumstances in Philippians 4, no expectation of a "fix" implied, but when we pour out anxiety to God, Jesus replaces that anxiety with peace that transcends all understanding. Even if a situation is beyond understanding, the lack of understanding does not hinder peace that can be received. Peace transcends or "trumps" understanding by the power of the gospel.

A parent who cannot understand why his teenager was killed in an auto accident can still experience peace. A wife who cannot comprehend her husband's irrational and repeated adulterous behavior can receive peace while remaining married. The employee who does not receive praise for a job well done can still experience the delight of inner peace that compels continued faithful work. The word cancer, spoken in the office of the oncologist, does not eliminate the possibility of peace. The stock market falling twenty percent in a few days cannot steal security from the one who pours out anxiety to the Savior. The peace of Christ transcends every circumstance and when the anxious heart is poured out to the personal Savior, peace will reign.

In *Deeper Places*, Matthew Jacoby says, "As we open our hearts to let out the pain, we thereby also open our hearts to receive consolation, and our consolation is God's preoccupation with restoration. . . . So it is that many of the most profound expressions of joy in the psalms arise in the midst of the most grievous circumstances." (Jacoby 62) This is the remarkable, redemptive result of pouring out the soul. The highest peace often follows the deepest despair not because circumstances changed but because the soul was emptied before God, who poured in the peace of his son.

I have grown to so appreciate God's peace that I rarely ask

him for a change of circumstances anymore, but for peace within that circumstance. Experiencing peace is one thing, but delighting in the peace of Christ that transcends tough circumstances is life-changing. Perhaps that is what enabled James to write, "Consider it pure joy, my brothers, whenever you face trials of many kinds," (Jas. 1:2) and Paul, who said, "we also rejoice in our sufferings" (Rom. 5:3a) or Peter, who encouraged us to "rejoice that you participate in the sufferings of Christ, so that you may be overjoyed when his glory is revealed" (1 Pet. 4:13). These men not only understood the power of peace but they also experienced peace that transcended understanding.

This transcending peace also guards the heart and mind in Christ Jesus against discouragement. Discouragement is one of the most insidious emotions the evil one uses against those who trust Jesus; but when discouragement is poured out, Jesus pours in the transcendent peace of his life that guards the heart and protects it from being held captive to negative and destructive emotions. Peace from the life of Christ that guards the heart encapsulates and insulates the soul from emotions that cripple and paralyze.

God gave more than peace to the prophet Elijah when he poured out his soul in 1 Kings 19. Elijah lived in a perilous time for a prophet of God. Wicked King Ahab and his wife Jezebel had killed the other prophets of God and had recently threatened Elijah. So Elijah fled for his life to the wilderness and from there poured out his heart to God. Elijah cried out that he'd been zealously obedient when it seemed the rest of the nation had rejected God. In a moment of desperation and transparency, Elijah poured out that he was the only one left and now Jezebel was trying to kill him. God empowered Elijah with a fresh sense of *perspective* (1 Kings 19:18), *perseverance* to "stay in the fight" (1 Kings 19:15a), renewed *purpose* (1 Kings 19:15b) and *power* to effect change (1 Kings 19:16-17).

After years of intentionally pouring out my heart, I can testify that God often gives me what He gave Elijah: perspective, perseverance, purpose and power. Rarely does God intervene and change my circumstances, but God always *changes me* when I pour out my soul to Him. The Spirit who forms the life of Christ in me changes my perspective to a Jesus perspective and empowers Jesus-like perseverance. Oswald Chambers said in *My Utmost for His Highest*, "It is not so true that prayer changes things as that prayer changes me and I change things" (Chambers August 28th). That is the power of the gospel and how the formation of the life of Christ in the heart of the believer eventually changes culture around the influential believer.

Craig, one of the guys in a weekly men's group with me, works at UPS. Things get chaotic on the packing line when several workers are sorting boxes in a small space. It is not unusual for someone to get whacked with an errantly thrown box. It happened to Craig one day—he got hit square on the back of the head with a box. Instantly, anger flared up in Craig. But nearly as quickly came the compulsion to pour out this frustration to Christ. Craig kept his composure and quietly poured out his thoughts and feelings to his Savior. He described an almost instantaneous peace that flooded his soul, replacing the frustration and urge to retaliate physically or verbally. Pouring out the heart to God frees us to respond to troubles and minor annoyances with grace and love instead of retaliation and anger. Craig's heart was strengthened by the life of Christ when he spontaneously poured it out to Jesus his Savior.

David's Example from the Psalms

Psalm 142 is one of David's many "pour-out" psalms: "I pour out my complaint before him; before him I tell my trouble. I cry to you, O LORD . . . Listen to my cry, for I am in desperate need . . ." (Ps. 142:2, 5a, 6a). David poured out his heart with intensity and from desperation. A glance at the descriptive heading of this psalm reveals David wrote it while in a cave, likely on the run and hiding from an enemy who was pursuing him. David's soul was profoundly troubled. He feared for his life. After pouring out his heart in verses 1-6, David declared the power of the gospel, "Then the righteous will gather about me because of your goodness to me" (Ps. 142:7b). There is hope in that last phrase, and even confidence. Nothing changed circumstantially, but something changed in David's soul when he poured it out to God. This "soul progression" from trouble and lament to peace and confidence is indicative of David's "pour-out" psalms.

David's progression of peace is clearly illustrated in Psalm 13, another context of profound stress for David. Analyze Psalm 13 by identifying feelings and thoughts David expressed. After each phrase listed below, write one or two feeling words that capture what David poured out to God.

How long, O Lord? Will you forget me forever?

How long will you hide your face from me?

How long must I wrestle with my thoughts?

. . . and every day have sorrow in my heart?

How long will my enemy triumph over me?

Look on me and answer, O Lord my God.

Give light to my eyes, or I will sleep in death;

my enemy will say, "I have overcome him,"

. . . and my foes will rejoice when I fall.

The list of words describing feelings and thoughts David poured out before God might include: loneliness, abandonment, isolation, rejection, confusion, indecision, sorrow, defeat, not being heard, despair, fear, failure and a bit of depression. We don't know the specific context of this psalm, but obviously David was experiencing major discouragement and stress. David was forthcoming with his thoughts and feelings, pouring ugly and accusatory thoughts to God.

But notice David's last thought in Psalm 13, "But I trust in your unfailing love; my heart rejoices in your salvation. I will sing to the LORD, for he has been good to me" (Ps. 13:5-6). David's heart progressed dramatically from the beginning of this psalm to the end. The very process of pouring out his heart to the Lord seemed to change him as peace from his Savior flooded his soul. David's heart rejoiced because he poured out his soul to God. The change of heart David expressed from verse 1 to verse 6 seems almost schizophrenic. David poured out intense negative emotion, but by the end of his writing, probably just a few minutes, his soul was rejoicing: "I will sing to the LORD, for he has been good to me!" Psalm 13 is a powerful illustration of the promise of Philippians 4:7 - peace that comes when we pour out our hearts to Jesus. Ponder Psalm 13 and the Savior to whom David poured out his heart. Follow the pattern of Psalm 13 and personalize it, pouring out your heart to Jesus.

David's psalms are personal journal entries of a heart poured out to God that progresses from trouble to peace. Contrast David's "pour-out" phrases in Psalm 6 with his statements of soul peace at the end of the psalm: "My soul is in anguish . . . I am worn out from groaning; all night long I flood my bed with weeping and drench my couch with tears. My eyes grow weak with sorrow. . ." (Ps. 6:3a, 6, 7a). But then at the end of the psalm. . . "the LORD has heard my weeping. The LORD has heard my cry for mercy; the LORD accepts my prayer. All my enemies will be ashamed and dismayed; they will turn back in sudden disgrace" (Ps. 6:8b, 9-10). David's soul changed by the time he finished writing the psalm. The man was either schizophrenic or God transformed his heart as he pondered affectively. Pouring out the soul to God results in personal transformation as the life of Christ forms in the heart that has been emptied.

The great reformer Martin Luther once said, "Fall on your knees, lift your eyes and hands toward heaven . . . and pour out your trouble with tears before God . . . God desires it, and it is his will, that you should pour out your trouble before him and not let it lie upon yourself, dragging it about with you and being chaffed and tortured by it" (Luther 208). Luther, who lived a busy life with incredible levels of stress, was not chaffed or tortured by his troubles because he poured out his heart to God. The gospel solution to the brokenness of the world that weighs us down, chaffing and torturing us, is to pour out the trouble to our Savior.

Words from another prophet of God during a desperate time in Israel's history, Habakkuk, illustrate the "fill" of pouring out the soul:

Though the fig tree does not bud and there are no

grapes on the vines; though the olive crop fails
and the fields produce no food, though there are
no sheep in the pen and no cattle in the stalls, yet
I will rejoice in the LORD; I will be joyful in God
my Savior. The Sovereign LORD is my strength;
he makes my feet like the feet of a deer, he
enables me to go on the heights. (Hab. 3:17-19)

Drought, famine, scarcity and death were all around, but
Habakkuk still was able to say, "I will rejoice in the LORD, I will
be joyful in God my Savior." Nothing changed externally for the
prophet after pouring out, but his heart certainly changed.
Habakkuk pushed through scarce circumstances by pouring out
his heart and God empowered him on to new heights!

Psalms 42 and 43 describe a spiritual appetite that is created
from pouring out the heart and pondering God. "My soul is
downcast within me [pouring out] therefore I will remember you
[ponder]" (Ps. 42:6a). These two activities of spiritual digestion
and pondering and pouring out create an insatiable appetite for
God, "As the deer pants for streams of water, so my soul pants
for you, O God. My soul thirsts for God, for the living God.
Where can I go and meet with God?" (Ps. 42:1-2). This is the cry
of a hungry but blessed soul that seeks life from God through
affective pondering and pouring out the heart to God. Pondering
helps us "taste and see that the Lord is good;" and when we trust
God enough to pour out our hearts to him, our spiritual appetites
will become voracious. These two activities of the heart render
believers "starving thirsty" for God!

How to Pour out the Heart

The soul or heart, often used interchangeably, can be thought
of as the center of the mind, will and emotions. So the heart
contains thoughts, decisions and emotions - the core of what we
think, feel and choose. Just as it is useful to write out deep
thoughts of God when pondering Him, so it is helpful to write
out thoughts, feelings and choices of the heart. A personal
journal is a great tool for pouring out the heart. The Bible is
God's heart revealed to me, and I like to think of a journal as my
heart revealed to God. I started the practice of journaling thirty-
five years ago. Today I have three bookshelves full of journals

that express my poured-out heart to God. My journals don't mean much to anyone else, but whenever I read a page, no matter how many years ago it was written, I instantly remember the context and the condition of my soul at that moment. It doesn't take long until I begin to read of God's faithfulness in response to my poured-out heart. The Bible is God's record of faithfulness to his people. My journals are a record of God's faithfulness to me that empowers me with fresh faith, confidence and the peace of Jesus no matter what I am currently facing.

Others, like Craig, the UPS worker I described earlier, report remarkably quick experiences of the peace of Christ quieting their hearts when they pour out. Husbands and wives in bad marriages report lasting peace and renewed energy to stay in the marriage and work toward reconciliation. One man in a small group with me, who pours out by writing down the expressions of his heart, recently shared, "Peace seems to come to my heart before I even get the pen on the paper." It is amazing how quickly the peace of Christ forms in the poured-out heart of the believer.

Of course, there are times when peace doesn't come immediately. Sometimes it is hard to articulate or even identify feelings and thoughts of the soul. On those occasions, the psalms can help capture feelings, thoughts and choices of the heart. Find a psalm with which you identify and allow that psalm to compel what you pour out. A list of "feeling words" may also be helpful when pouring out. (Appendix B) Such a list can help identify what's going on in your soul so it can be expressed to the Lord Jesus. I have learned to pour out more frequently during more stressful seasons of life. Under stress, peace dissipates and I feel spiritually nauseous. When dealing with intense stress, pouring out once or twice is not enough. Longer term experiences of pouring out have taught me a wonderful blessing that I like to call the "Meatloaf Factor."

Remember the meatloaf sandwich story at the beginning of this chapter? That experience negatively imprinted me. To this day, years later, I cannot and will not eat a meatloaf sandwich. Those who study these things label the phenomenon as an illness-induced food aversion. Think about that spiritually. Several intense sessions of pouring out some "toxin" in the soul will create an aversion, a desire to stay clear of that toxin in the future. If what was ingested into the soul caused long-term stress and spiritual nausea, the soul will create a defense mechanism, just as the body does, as an aversion to ever doing that again. For example, if a child offends his mother by criticizing a meal she worked hours to prepare and mom reacts by sending the child to his room without supper, the boy will not be as quick to criticize the next meal. Pouring out pain teaches. Repeated pouring out is awkward, painful and messy, but it does create an aversion to repeating behavior that caused the trouble.

Pouring out the soul is one of the great gifts of God that has been ignored by Christians, particularly in the west. The songs of slaves in America, known as spirituals, are wonderful examples of pouring out the heart; but those songs, sung often in a dark period of our history, are rarely expressed today. Perhaps we feel little need to pour out because we are comfortable most of the time. It is time to recapture the beautiful and joyful experience of pouring out the heart to God. It's scary at first, and always messy, but persevere in pouring out. What lies ahead of you is peace, the wonderful peace of Christ taking form within you that empowers confidence, joy and perseverance.

Craig, my UPS friend who was whacked in the back of the head with a box, struggled to manage his anger for years. Craig said of pouring out, "I doubted that pouring out my heart would do any good. The box incident changed that." Now Craig is applying the principle of pouring out his heart intentionally and spontaneously while growing in transcendent peace. Trusting Jesus enough to pour out his heart to him is transforming Craig's life, marriage and parenting.

My wife Lanita and I have been pouring out our souls to God for thirty-five years of married life. When we feel disappointment or anger, instead of venting on one another we've learned to pour it out to Jesus. Ephesians 4:26 teaches us to not let the sun go down on our anger, but it doesn't say we should vent on each other. Venting vertically through pouring out to Jesus has saved us from many conflicts. When we accept God's invitation and pour out our negative feelings to Him, our ability to resolve conflict is not hindered by raw, critical emotion. We can then move toward one another in the peace of Christ and resolve the issue. So when I feel anger toward my wife, I refuse to speak it to her until I have first poured it out to Christ and received his peace. Usually the Lord transforms my heart and the anger goes away, along with the potential conflict. Sometimes this takes a few "pour-out" sessions over a period of days or even weeks but, eventually, when all the anger is poured out on Jesus, I am able to approach my wife with the peace of Christ and resolve the conflict.

My wife pours out to Jesus as I do. Sometimes she'll ask if I want to read her journal. I'm scared to read her journal. Anyone who knows my beautiful, gentle, positive wife would be startled to read what feelings she pours out to God about me. But once her anger is poured out on him, the life of Christ fills her afresh and she beautifully reflects Christ to me. She doesn't stuff her anger, nor do I; we choose to let Jesus deal with it. We reconcile quickly because we move to solution side about the real issue instead being stuck in the intense, negative emotion that surrounds the issue. The peace and life of Christ at the center of our relationship resolves conflict before it intensifies.

In summary, remember the following when pouring out your heart to Jesus:

1. Pouring includes confessing sin, circumstances, stress, conflict and pressure.
2. Pour out your thoughts, feelings and decisions, both positive and negative.
3. Express what you pour out by writing in a journal.
4. Repeatedly pour out stresses, hurts and sins that recur.
5. Use scripture as a mirror for your soul to compel you to pour out.
6. Vent to God, not to others, through pouring out.

Imagine how the church would shine in the world if believers would vent their anger and frustration with one another on a loving Savior, who replaces frustration with peace and forms his life within empty souls. Vertically venting is a powerful testimony of faith that will positively influence others and transform relationships. It is part of a natural overflow that comes when we empty ourselves of ourselves and swallow the Spirit of the living Christ, as we'll discover in the next chapter. Lane and Tripp describe it this way in *How People Change*:

Scripture's approach calls us to forsake the things we have sought to fill our emptiness. Before we can be filled with God's grace, we must engage in intelligent, honest repentance . . . Repentance is a form of emptying the heart . . . Along with deep repentance, scripture calls us to faith that rests and feeds upon the living Christ. He fills us with himself through the person of the Holy Spirit and our hearts are transformed by faith. (Lane and Tripp 23)

Following is a letter I wrote to our congregation after three tragic shootings in three years, all within our congregation. The first was a senior high youth worker who committed suicide; the second, a year later, a middle school boy in our youth group shot and killed another middle school boy in our youth group; and the third, about two years later, a mother from our congregation shot her fifteen-year-old son while he lay sleeping in bed early on a Sunday morning. I wrote:

The tragic events of last Sunday morning are traumatic reminders of why we so desperately need Jesus. I have, at times, felt emotionally nauseous when thinking about what happened and the shootings within our body over the past few years. As I poured out my faint and disturbed heart to our Lord this week, I found understanding and comfort in the book of Lamentations. In his affliction, Jeremiah found strength and hope in God through pouring out the pain and anguish of his heart (lamentations).

Lamentations 3 reveals God's righteous anger and justified discipline in response to human sin but also proclaims God's goodness, love and faithfulness to us, his sinful people. Pondering the following truths of God revealed there may encourage you, as well:
- God has SEEN and HEARD all that is wrong in our world and hearts
- God's sovereign reign ENDURES even when

evil seems to rule
- God REDEEMS life
- God's MERCIES are new every morning
- God pours out his fierce ANGER on his own son
- God comes NEAR to us when we cry out to him

Only the gospel power of Jesus Christ can redeem such tragedy. Let us, the people of Crossroads Church, join together in praying to that redemptive end as we seek our Lord for comfort and petition him for peace of the Spirit in time of awful tragedy.

Pouring out our souls to Jesus brings peace, nourishment from God that empowers us forward as it did David. But because Jesus was broken and poured out, God has more for us than even David received. In the next chapter we'll focus on the living water of the Holy Spirit, whom God pours out freely through his broken and poured-out Son. The Holy Spirit is God's greatest gift, the completeness of satisfaction, indeed, the fullness of life. But God does not force his life on us. He pours out his Spirit in Christ, but we must desire to receive. Our desire is expressed through asking, petition—a specific ask. Chapter 5 will equip and encourage you to petition. David did not ask for the personal presence of God to form within him because it wasn't available to him, but it is to you in Christ. Ask and you will receive.

QUESTIONS FOR THOUGHT AND INTERACTION
Chapter 4

1. Read Psalm 6. List feeling words that describe what David poured out. Circle any feeling words with which you identify.

2. Write out other expressions of your soul prompted by this psalm. Share some of what you poured out.

3. What are some "bad meat" thoughts or feelings that frequent your soul in a typical week?

4. Describe some times when off-loading your heart to someone else has reduced your stress level.

5. What is the hardest thing for you in vomiting your soul? Why do you think that's so?

6. How can we encourage each other to pour out our souls?

7. What are some potentially harmful side effects of pouring out our souls to others instead of on God?

8. Make a list of words that describe feelings, thoughts, or choices to use when pouring out your soul to God.

9. How does using a journal as a "soul vomit" book change any thoughts or feelings you may have had about journaling?

Chapter 5
Petition the Spirit

"We were all given the one Spirit to drink"
(1 Corinthians 12:13)

A predictable outcome of pouring out is thirst. Pouring out leaves the heart dry and empty. Body and soul crave water to replenish fluids and get the digestive process moving again. A little water won't do; body and soul need major replenishment of fluids. The poured-out soul craves one thing, living water from God, the Holy Spirit. As believers in Christ become more faithful in pouring out their souls, the Church will experience a great craving for the Holy Spirit which will, I trust, compel renewal. A healthy human body is about sixty percent fluid; a healthy soul is one hundred percent life of Christ.

Jesus met a desperately empty woman one day at an old well in a place called Sychar. The woman was there to draw water from the well and Jesus asked her to give Him a drink. The woman's defensive response was indicative of her emptiness: "You are a Jew and I am a Samaritan woman. How can you ask me for a drink?" (John 4:9). The prejudice between Jews and Samaritans had begun hundreds of years earlier when the Assyrians deported the Jews from their homeland and replaced them with foreigners to settle and care for the land. 2 Kings 17:24b-25a says, "They [the foreigners or Samaritans] took over Samaria and lived in its towns. When they first lived there they did not worship the LORD." Generations of ensuing prejudice is what caused the Samaritan woman to be so surprised at Jesus' request. In addition to the ethnic prejudice, gender prejudice usually kept a man from talking publicly with a woman in that culture. The story later reveals the woman had been married five times and was now living with a man to whom she was not married. Bitter prejudice, rejection and failure drove this Samaritan woman to try and fill her soul's emptiness with what a man could give her.

Jesus offered living water to this desperate woman. "Everyone who drinks this water [the water from the world's well] will be thirsty again, but whoever drinks the water I give him will never thirst. Indeed, the water I give him will become in him a spring of water welling up to eternal life" (John 4:13-14). Lasting satisfaction can only be found in the living water of the Spirit—water that satisfies the soul: "If anyone is thirsty, let him come to me and drink. Whoever believes in me, as the Scripture has said, streams of living water will flow from within him. By this he meant the Spirit, whom those who believe in him were later to receive" (John 7:37b-39a).

Living water is the primary metaphor in the Bible to help us understand the Holy Spirit. Jeremiah 2:13, which warns people against other sources of water, describes God as a spring of living water: "My people have forsaken me, the spring of living water, and have dug their own cisterns, broken cisterns that cannot hold water." Since Eden, men and women have attempted to fill their souls with everything but God. We dig our own cisterns, but they cannot hold water. Self-excavated cisterns cannot satisfy the deep thirst of the soul.

THE FOUNTAIN OF LIFE

Psalm 36:8-9a, "They feast on the abundance of your house; you give them drink from your river of delights. For with you is the fountain of life." God is a fountain or spring of living water that never runs dry. Author John Piper has some interesting insight into this descriptive metaphor of God:

> God is a mountain spring, not a watering trough.
> A mountain spring is self-replenishing. It constantly overflows and supplies others . . . So if you want to glorify the worth of a spring you do it by getting down on your hands and knees and drinking to your heart's satisfaction, until you have the refreshment and strength to go back down in the valley and tell people what you've found . . . Since that is the way God is, we are not surprised to learn from Scripture that the way to please God is to come to him to get and not to give, to drink and not to water. He is most glorified in us when we are most satisfied in him. (*The Pleasures of God* 216)

We honor God by going to him in desperation and drinking to satisfy our souls. God's nature is grace, so he is always giving unconditionally. He gives and gives just like a mountain spring that never runs dry. Since God is complete in himself, he will never be deficient, even though he is constantly giving. Isaiah 58:11, "The LORD will guide you always; he will satisfy your needs in a sun-scorched land and will strengthen your frame. You will be like a well–watered garden, like a spring whose waters never fail." When the Spirit of God is swallowed by the soul, even the driest cracks and darkest recesses of the heart are replenished; but without "moisture from God" the heart dries up and becomes brittle, fractured, splintered, damaged, fruitless and hardened.

Ezekiel 37 uses even more vivid imagery to describe a dry and dead people. Ezekiel saw a valley full of dry, brittle human bones that represented the "whole house of Israel" (Ez. 37:3b). God asked the prophet if such bones could live. Ezekiel replied, "O Sovereign LORD, you alone know." God demonstrated to Ezekiel that life could again come to those old brittle bones if the Spirit of God flowed. When the Spirit came the bones rattled. Tendons and ligaments appeared and connected bone to bone. Fluid-filled muscle appeared on the newly connected bones, followed by living flesh, until people stood with new life. God ended his graphic lesson to Ezekiel with these words, "I will put my Spirit in you and you will live" (Ezek. 37:14a). God's Spirit, swallowed into the human soul, brings life to dismembered people with parched, brittle hearts.

The Samaritan woman, like all of us, searched and longed for authentic, unconditional love. But, like so many of us, the Samaritan couldn't find love in marriage, ethnic identity, gender roles or even in traditional forms of worship. Jesus taught her the only love that truly satisfies is the love of God's Spirit. "God has poured out his love into our hearts by the Holy Spirit" (Rom. 5:5b). God's love pours forth as a fountain of life that will never run dry.

When your soul is empty and you've tried everything, but still your soul is dry and parched, when you've poured it all out and need to be replenished, turn to the Lord Jesus, who will lead you to living water. "For the Lamb at the center of the throne [Jesus] will be their shepherd; he will lead them to springs of living water" (Rev. 7:17). Since the finished work of Christ's life, death, resurrection and ascension, the Spirit has been made personally available to all who believe. Feeding is believing and so is drinking. Drinking in the Spirit of Christ is a privilege Old Testament believers did not experience (Heb. 11:13, 39-40). King David's instructive example of feeding on the Lord is insufficient at this point. We must now look to the New Testament to understand the fullness of the gospel and the life God desires to form in us.

Receiving the Spirit

"And you also were included in Christ when you heard the word of truth, the gospel of your salvation. Having believed, you were marked in him with a seal, the promised Holy Spirit" (Eph. 1:13). When personal faith takes hold of what God has given in Christ, God dispenses the Holy Spirit into the soul of the believer. From the moment of regeneration, the Spirit resides in the soul of the believer who trusts in Christ. Those who have the Spirit residing in them know it: "This is how we know that he lives in us; We know it by the Spirit he gave us" (1 John 3:24b). It is the Spirit of God who fills the believer with the life of Christ. When God pours in his Spirit (Tit. 3:5-6) and actually dwells in the souls of believers everything changes. John spoke of this amazing reality in his first letter, "We know that we live in him and he in us, because he has given us of his Spirit. . . . If anyone acknowledges that Jesus is the Son of God, God lives in him and he in God" (1 John 4:13, 15). This is the life-giving, transformational reality of the gospel. The gospel is the actual presence of the Spirit of God dwelling in the human soul. The Holy Spirit is not a metaphor or a symbol of some ethereal spiritual experience, not just an abstract force or power; he is a living being. When the Holy Spirit indwells a believer he crucifies the flesh and takes control of the soul (Rom. 8:9b-10). And so the life of Christ begins to form in the believer.

Evangelical theology of the Spirit life dwelling in the souls of believers is embraced by millions, and yet so few seem to experience the satisfaction and delight of the Spirit. I like to ask people to assign a number from one through ten that describes their personal awareness of and experience with the Holy Spirit, ten representing what Romans 8:6b describes, "the mind controlled by the Spirit is life and peace" and one representing what Acts 19:2b says, "we have not even heard that there is a Holy Spirit." The most common number cited to describe personal experience of the Spirit is between two and four. This ought not be! Peter taught that God wants everyone who repents and believes to experience the indwelling Spirit. (Acts 2:38) Why, then, do so many believers rank their experience of the Spirit with the number two or three?

Many think of the Spirit as a gift given only at the moment of new birth. New believers gladly receive the Spirit when they first believe but fail to grow in the Spirit and soon wonder whether the Spirit ever did indwell them. What happened? Did the Spirit leave them? Was their conversion experience not authentic? Is there something more they need to do to experience fullness of the Spirit? This line of questioning represents a common frustration in the souls of thousands of believers, causing many to misunderstand the Holy Spirit and despair in their pursuit of him.

Receiving the Holy Spirit should be continuous, like drinking water. To drink of the Holy Spirit at the moment of new birth but never again creates spiritual dehydration. Think about that. No human being could live to say, "The last drink of water I had was over a year ago and I've felt great ever since." Without fluids, death comes in a few days. The body must be continually replenished with water and so must the soul. Drinking once of the Spirit is simply not sufficient for soul satisfaction or the formation of Christ's life within. Andrew Murray wrote in *Experiencing the Holy Spirit*, "The fullness of the Spirit is not a gift that is given once for all as a part of the heavenly life. It is rather a constantly flowing stream of the river of the water of life that issues from beneath the throne of God and of the Lamb" (74). That's why Jesus taught us in John 6:54 and 56 to drink of Him in the present continuous sense. "Whoever eats my flesh and drinks my blood has eternal life, and I will raise him up at the last day. Whoever eats my flesh and drinks my blood remains in me and I in him." The word "drinks" in these verses is in the present tense, meaning continuous, ongoing action. Drinking in the Spirit of Jesus is not a one-time thing but an ongoing experiencing of swallowing the Spirit into our souls as we swallow water into our digestive systems.

Petition in the Spirit

"Do not get drunk on wine, which leads to debauchery. Instead, be filled with the Spirit" (Eph. 5:18). We are to be full— not with the world's drink or satisfaction—but full of the Spirit of God. The verb "be filled" is a command or imperative. It's non-optional for the believer. The verb is stated in the present tense, which means it is an ongoing thing: be filled and continue being filled. Finally, the verb "be filled" is in the passive voice as opposed to active. If it were in the active voice I could fill myself with the Spirit, but since it is a passive verb I must trust someone or something else to fill me. Now think about Jesus' metaphor of drinking. When I'm thirsty, I take hold of a glass of water, pour it into my mouth, swallow and the water fills me. When I drink of the Spirit, I am more of a passive recipient because I don't pour the Spirit in, God does. Swallowing while someone else pours the liquid into me requires trust, but even with trust in the one pouring, swallowing what someone else pours can be a bit awkward and messy. The key is the commitment of the one swallowing. Once swallowing starts, it shouldn't stop or there will be a mess. That's what Paul is teaching in Ephesians 5:18 - never stop drinking in the Spirit. God does the pouring, we do the swallowing.

Jesus encouraged the Samaritan woman to continuously drink of living water. Jesus' words to her in John 4:14, "whoever drinks the water I give him will never thirst" cannot mean a one-time drink, because that is inconsistent with Jesus' present continuous tense of drinking in John 6 and Paul's command to be continually filled from Ephesians 5:18. Jesus was telling the woman that if she continually drank the living water he offered her, she would never need to ingest anything else into her soul, because his living water will continually satisfy. Since the cross of Jesus, the fountain of living water is continually flowing to those who will drink of it by faith in Christ.

So how does it happen? How does the Spirit continually fill the believer? We've already seen that God is a fountain, continuously pouring out life, but not everyone receives the Spirit

God pours out because it requires faith— believing is drinking or swallowing. So how does the human heart swallow what God pours out in Christ? Jesus said it clearly in Luke 11:13b, "How much more will your Father in heaven give the Holy Spirit to those who ask him?" We have to ask to appropriate what God is pouring out in Christ. Asking is the beginning of the heart's "swallow." When a believer in Christ asks to be filled with the Spirit, God pours the Spirit into that believer's soul. Some may feel receiving the Spirit cannot be as simple as just asking for it, as if Jesus intended to say something else in Luke 11:13, but a brief study of the surrounding context affirms that Jesus compels us to ask for the Holy Spirit and, when we ask, God will give.

Luke 11 begins with Jesus praying in a certain place. When he finished praying, one of the disciples asked, "Lord, teach us to pray, just as John taught his disciples" (Luke 11:1b). Jesus then speaks what we know as the Lord's Prayer, but goes on to tell a parable of a person who is both bold and persistent in asking for specific help. The point of the parable is that the giver responds positively to a persistent and bold petition. Jesus then followed the parable with further instruction on the specifics of prayer:

> Ask and it will be given to you . . . For everyone
> who asks receives. . . Which of you fathers, if your
> son asks for a fish, will give him a snake instead?
> Or if he asks for an egg, will give him a scorpion?
> If you then, though you are evil, know how to
> give good gifts to your children, how much more
> will your Father in heaven give the Holy Spirit to
> those who ask him! (Luke 11:9-13)

Ask and the Spirit will be given you because your father is a giver of good gifts (Jas. 1:17). Which of his gifts would God want us to have more than his Spirit?

In the Lord's Prayer, Jesus implored his disciples to pray for God's kingdom to come on earth (Luke 11:2b), and how will the kingdom advance on earth except by the Spirit? Praying specifically to be filled with the Spirit is the way the kingdom advances on earth, as those who trust the King become his ambassadors, overflowing with the life and power of the Spirit to the world around them. Be bold and persistent in asking to receive the Holy Spirit. Swallow the Spirit God is pouring out to you by asking to be filled.

Why wouldn't the Father give the Spirit to those who ask him? That was the plan from the beginning. The Holy Spirit is part of the mysterious gift of the gospel the ancients longed for (Heb. 11:13, 39) but could not receive because Jesus had not yet been glorified (John 7:39). Even earthly fathers love their children enough to give them the good things they ask for without being stingy. Why would God withhold his Spirit? Of course God will give the great gift of the Holy Spirit to those who ask. God wants believers in Christ to be indwelt with the very essence of God, the Living Water of the universe that can form the life of Christ in them, but God doesn't force feed us - that's really important. We call it "free will," and God created us with it. God gives lavishly and graciously, but we must ask. Think of asking not as a condition of getting, but simply as the reception of God's gift. God pours out his Spirit unconditionally and abundantly to those who ask.

Jesus made the necessity of asking quite clear to the Samaritan woman, "If you knew the gift of God and who it is that asks you for a drink, you would have asked him and he would have given you living water" (John 4:10). Jesus mentioned three conditions for receiving living water: 1. Know the gift (Holy Spirit) 2. Know the giver (Jesus) 3. ASK. There is no receiving without asking. James said, "You do not have because you do not ask" (James 4:2). Jesus said, "Ask and you will receive."

Jesus' mother, Mary, experienced the power of asking in John 2 at the wedding in Cana. Although Mary didn't specifically ask for Jesus to turn water into wine, she clearly presented her problem to Jesus with the expectation he would help. Jesus reluctantly performed the first of many miracles because Mary's ask compelled him. There is no textual evidence to suggest that Jesus would have performed that miracle had Mary not expressed expectation of help.

In John Chapters 14-16, the most explicit instruction about the Holy Spirit in all of scripture, the word "ask" is used twelve times by Jesus. "Ask and you will receive, and your joy will be complete" (John 16:24). The use of the word "ask" in these chapters is in relation to receiving from God. Since Luke 11:13 makes it clear that God will give the Holy Spirit to those who ask,

93

much of our lack of experience of the Holy Spirit is probably due to a lack of asking. God is pouring out his Spirit in Christ, but he's not pushing the Spirit "intravenously" to us. We are passive recipients according to Ephesians 5:18, but we must still ask because God doesn't force his life on us.

Asking is each individual believer's responsibility. No one else can do it for you, just as no one else can swallow for you. Swallowing or drinking in the Spirit of Jesus is synonymous with asking. When a believer asks to be filled with the Spirit, he is opening his empty, poured out heart to receive what God wants to pour in, the Holy Spirit. The soul's first swallow occurs at the beginning of the faith journey, but to experience ongoing satisfaction and the formation of Christ's life within, the believer must continue to ask. John R. W. Stott describes this in his classic book, *Baptism and Fullness*:

> We are not only to come to Jesus once, in penitence and faith, but also thereafter to keep coming and to keep drinking, because we keep thirsting. We do that physically. Whenever we are thirsty, we get a drink. We must learn to do it spiritually also. The Christian is a spiritual dipsomaniac, always thirsty, always drinking. And drinking is not asking for water, but actually taking it. It is extremely simple. Drinking is one of the first activities which babies learn; indeed they do it by instinct. (54)

We must learn to swallow the Spirit. The soul's drink begins with asking and then swallowing what God pours out.

It's not a new concept—it's always been this way with God and those who believe in Him. God is a fountain of living water; always has been. The only reason we fail to receive the Spirit is because we don't ask God on a continual basis. God is already pouring out his Spirit but to swallow the Spirit you must ask. When your soul thirsts, ask God for a drink of His Spirit. The Holy Spirit is not just a deposit guaranteeing our salvation as Ephesians 1:14 reminds us, but the ongoing fountain of living, satisfying water from God that quenches the thirst of the soul and forms the life of Christ within. Receiving the Spirit at the moment of new birth is the first drink of the soul but not the last.

It is the first of many to come, so eat, drink, feast! Be full and satisfied in the Lord Jesus.

Pouring out the soul is a necessary prerequisite to swallowing the fullness of the Spirit because the contents of the sinful heart are incompatible with the Spirit - the two cannot co-exist in the same space. Andrew Murray points out the important connection of "swallowing in the Spirit" with pouring out the heart:

> Your own life and the life of God cannot fill the heart at the same time. Your life hinders the entrance of the life of God. When your own life is cast out, the life of God will fill you. As long as I myself am still something, Jesus Himself cannot be everything. My life must be expelled, then the Spirit of Jesus will flow in. . . . You must utterly lose that life [the life that finds delight in self and the world] before the full life of the Spirit of God can be yours. (*Experiencing the Holy Spirit* 54)

When we neglect to pour out and empty our souls to God we leave insufficient room in our souls for the fullness of the Spirit. But when believers in Christ "cast out their life," the Spirit flows into the empty heart when asked. It's a kind of "spiritual gravity."

This principle of water filling empty space is illustrated in creation by fluids seeking their own level due to gravity. It's how a water tower works. Water is pumped high up into the tower above faucets in homes that draw from the tower. Since the water faucet is at a significantly lower elevation than the water in the tower, the water that comes out of the faucet comes fast or under pressure since water seeks its own level. But, if the water pipe that feeds the faucet becomes clogged at any point along the line, no water will come out of the faucet. That pipe needs to be cleaned out and the clog removed before water can flow out of the faucet. As long as there are no restrictions and the pipeline remains connected (John 15), water will flow.

Human souls are clogged with sin, guilt and other restrictors to the flow of the Spirit, but when a believer pours these things out, the soul is empty; and when that empty soul asks, it is filled with the living water of God's Spirit. When a believing soul asks, it's as if "Spirit gravity" takes over and fills the empty heart connected to God in Christ. A soul that continually asks (Eph. 5:18, Luke 11:13) is "pressurized" by living water and will be filled as soon as it is emptied. That's why the poured-out soul experiences peace almost immediately. Stay connected to Christ, empty yourself, (pour out your heart), ask, swallow and receive the continuous gift of filling from God.

An interesting picture of this "Spirit gravity" is found in the writings of the prophet Zechariah. In Chapter 4, verses 2-3, the prophet sees a picture of a large bowl on top of a lamp stand with seven oil-fed lamps attached to the bowl. The bowl served as a reservoir of oil that flowed down into the lamps to keep them burning. Next to the bowl of oil were two olive trees that had branches that hung out over the open bowl. The olive trees dripped oil constantly into the bowl, which kept it full of oil and subsequently kept the lamps burning. Not only did the reservoir of oil keep the lamps supplied with oil, but that oil came to the lamps with gravity-fed pressure so that the lamps burned consistently and brightly without flickering. God desires His people to be well supplied, brightly burning lamps fed by the continual flow of His Spirit. So let your light shine among men! Let the light of Christ being formed in you shine forth continually.

The believer connected to God will be automatically supplied by "Spirit gravity" whenever he pours out or empties his soul and asks to be filled. Through this vital connection to the eternal source of living water, swallowing the Spirit becomes as natural as swallowing water. It is hard not to swallow the Spirit. Bev, a woman in our congregation, described it this way, "I don't understand how my digestive system knows what to do when I swallow something, but it does. All I have to do is take a bite of food and it goes to work. I don't have to make it happen. I don't have to feel it happen. It just happens." The Spirit is that way. When you feed on God's precious promises and 'swallow' them into your spirit by saying, 'I believe, I receive,' the Spirit is released. You don't have to make it happen. You don't have to feel it happen. It just happens.

Think again about Jesus' metaphor of the vine and branches in John 15. As long as a branch stays connected to the vine, that branch will bear fruit. Think about how a branch bears fruit. Fruit is mostly fluid that comes from sap that flows through the vine. How does the sap get from the vine to the fruit? It flows through the branch. For this to happen, the branch must remain connected to the vine. As long as it's connected, the life-giving sap will flow from the vine, to and through the branch, and eventually become the juice of the fruit. The way that sap gets from the vine to the branch is the idea of swallowing the Spirit. It's all about the connection, the flow of "Spirit gravity" and a healthy branch without internal obstructions.

> We are like a branch that is already filled with the sap of the vine and is crying for the continued and increasing flow of that sap. Just as the branch needs more sap to bring its fruit to perfection, the believer, rejoicing in the possession of the Spirit, still thirsts and cries for more. . . . The Greek word for receiving and taking is the same. When Jesus said, 'Everyone that asks, receives,' he used the same verb as at the Last Supper— 'take and eat'. . . . One thing we can be sure of is that the Father desires to have us filled with His Spirit." (*With Christ in the School of Prayer* 56-57)

Ask and receive, take and eat, swallow and consume Christ. Meditate on these multiple metaphors: a branch taking in sap, a gravity-fed oil lamp and how water moves to and flows in the body. Thinking on these metaphors will equip, inspire and compel you to be filled with the Spirit of God. This is God's desire for you and gift to you. What an amazing privilege it is to be filled and empowered by the actual presence of God's Spirit. God did not give us these metaphors just to get us to think deeper about an obscure, mystical concept, but rather that we might ingest his Spirit and discover life that he forms in us. "I no longer live, but Christ lives in me. The life I live in the body, I live by faith in the Son of God, who loved me and gave himself for me" (Gal. 2:20). Paul lived by the Spirit of Christ in him. Paul poured his life out that he might gain Christ under the pressure of "Spirit gravity." "I consider everything a loss compared to the surpassing greatness of knowing Christ Jesus my Lord, for whose sake I have lost all things. I consider them rubbish, that I may gain Christ" (Phil. 3:8). The only life that interested Paul was the life of Christ being formed within him.

Eugene Peterson's paraphrase of Romans 8 from the Message is helpful:

> Those who trust God's action in them find that God's Spirit is in them—living and breathing God! Obsession with self in these matters is a dead end; attention to God leads us out into the open, into a spacious, free life . . . If God himself has taken up residence in your life, you can hardly be thinking more of yourself than of him. Anyone, of course, who has not welcomed this invisible but clearly present God, the Spirit of Christ, won't know what we're talking about. But for you who welcome him, in whom he dwells— even though you still experience all the limitations of sin—you yourself experience life on God's terms. It stands to reason, doesn't it, that if the alive—and—present God who raised Jesus from the dead moves into your life, he'll do the same thing in you that he did in Jesus, bringing you alive to himself? When God lives and breathes in you (and he does, as surely as he did in Jesus), you are delivered from that dead life. With his Spirit living in you, your body will be as alive as Christ's is! (*The Message* Rom. 8:6-13)

This is the life God wants for you, the Spirit-filled life which comes through connection with Christ. The Spirit-filled life is a life controlled by the Spirit of God, not the self, because self has been poured out.

Ponder with me an incredible picture of living water from Ezekiel 47:1-12. The sea referred to in Ezekiel 47 is the Dead Sea. It's named the Dead Sea because it cannot support any organic life with the exception of some bacteria and other microbes. The salt concentration of the Dead Sea is 33%, the highest of any body of water on earth. The Great Salt Lake in Utah is only 22% salt and the oceans 3%. The Dead Sea has several inlets, but no outlets, other than evaporation, so it is stagnant—a lifeless body of water. Evaporation, in addition to human water diversion, is significant enough that the water level of the sea is sinking about one meter every year, causing the shores of the Dead Sea to be the lowest dry ground on the planet—some 417 meters below sea level. The Jordan River flows into the north end of the Dead Sea, and where the sea and river meet, dead fish litter the banks. The contaminates in the Dead Sea make survival impossible for fish swimming downstream. Although rich in minerals and beautiful in its own unique way, the Dead Sea cannot support life.

Ezekiel 47 also describes a flow of water coming from the temple of God. The little stream of water Ezekiel saw grew larger and larger until it became "a river that no one could cross" (47:5). Ezekiel describes how on the banks of the river a great number of fruit trees grew, saying, "their leaves will not wither, nor will their fruit fail. Every month they will bear, because the water from the sanctuary flows to them. Their fruit will serve for food and their leaves for healing" (47:12). The picture is a river that supports life and enables flourishing fruit. Ezekiel 47:8b says, "When it [the river water] empties into the Sea [the Dead Sea], the water there becomes fresh." Think about that! What an amazing illustration of the power of living water. Verse 9b says, ". . .where the river flows everything will live." The living water of God's Spirit has power to purify and bring life where there was only death. "Swarms of living creatures will live wherever the river flows. There will be large numbers of fish, because this water flows there and makes the salt water fresh." (Ezek. 47:9). Life abounds anywhere near this river. Wherever the living water of God's Spirit flows there is life. God's Spirit is and gives life.

Compare the contents of the Dead Sea with the contents of your soul. What life-threatening minerals abound in your soul? Are you 33% concentrated with "lifeless minerals?" Even if your soul is only 3% concentration of minerals, like the oceans, it still cannot support life as God intended. We enter the world with souls contaminated by the minerals of sin. The effects of the world and the evil one who operates here contaminate our souls all the more until our souls, like the Dead Sea, cannot support life. But our loving God comes to us as a river of life-giving, refreshing water. When a poured-out soul swallows the living water of God, life begins to form where there was only death.

Where the river flows, everything will live! Where the river flows, the life of Christ is formed.

So how do I swallow the Spirit?

There are no steps to swallowing the Spirit, any more than there are steps to swallowing water, but it is instructive to consider what is involved in swallowing water as a point of comparison to swallowing the Spirit. First, swallowing doesn't happen against the will of the one swallowing; neither is the Spirit received against one's will. God pours out his Spirit, but that Spirit must be willfully received by spiritual swallowing—swallowing is believing. God doesn't force his Spirit upon us. Rather, the desired Spirit is received willfully upon asking. So asking for the Spirit is like swallowing. This may be awkward to think about but Jesus affirmed that upon asking, the Spirit is received: "If you then, though you are evil, know how to give good gifts to your children, how much more will your Father in heaven give the Holy Spirit to those who ask him!" (Luke 11:13). God will not withhold something as precious as his Spirit to those who sincerely desire and ask for it. Jesus' death on the cross paved the way for us to receive the Spirit, but you have to ask!

Jesus made it clear to the Samaritan woman in John 4 that to receive the living water of the Spirit required three things: 1) Know the gift—John 4:10a 2) Know the giver—John 4:10b 3) Ask—John 4:10c. Upon one's asking, Jesus promised to give the Holy Spirit - John 4:10d, the ultimate satisfaction of the soul. Perhaps some are unfamiliar with the gift of the Holy Spirit or with the giver, Jesus. More common may be people who know the gift but fail to consistently swallow by simply asking and receiving in the name of Jesus.

Second, it's impossible to swallow and talk at the same time. Perhaps we don't swallow the Spirit because we are too busy talking, working, advancing our agenda or doing our own thing. In Psalm 46:10 it appears that God is speaking more to David than through David when the Spirit says, "Be still, and know that I am God;" God is encouraging David to not speak but to quiet his mouth and soul before God. The result: David declares it in the next verse, "The LORD Almighty is with us" (Ps. 46:11a).

Isn't that interesting? "Be still and know that I am God" and what will follow is a certainty of God's presence.

Quieting the soul of speech, thought, busyness, worry, stress and anxiety is critical to receiving the Spirit. That is why pouring out the soul is so vital to the process of spiritual nutrition; it quiets our hearts before God, enabling us to "swallow" the Spirit God pours out to us. Jesus' instruction about denying and losing oneself is the ultimate in pouring out and is a prerequisite to fullness of the Spirit.

A third unique thing about swallowing is that it's hard to stop once you've started. Once swallowing has been initiated, it is not easy to shut down without a mess. Swallowing the Spirit takes commitment to continue receiving the Spirit God gives. This is the continual drink of the soul that Paul teaches in Ephesians 5:18b, "Be filled with the Spirit." Swallowing is an ongoing guzzle of the soul or asking to receive the Holy Spirit. Persevere in swallowing the Spirit even if you don't completely understand how to do it. As you ask and continue to drink, the understanding and experience of receiving the Spirit will become more vital as the life of Christ forms within you.

Many fail to live in the fullness of the Spirit because they stop asking for the Spirit (Jas. 4:2b-3). Never stop swallowing (asking for) the Holy Spirit. Our evangelical obsession with the "prayer of accepting Jesus" hinders our ongoing swallowing of God's Spirit. Those who recite some prayer of acceptance mistakenly think that one ask is sufficient for fullness of the Spirit; but that is not consistent with Ephesians 5:18 or Jesus' instruction about drinking in living water.

Finally, we swallow because experience has taught us that swallowing quenches thirst. Swallowing the Spirit quenches thirst by replenishing the entire poured-out soul with the life of Christ - mind, will and emotions. Just as pondering God is a function of the entire heart and pouring out is emptying the mind, will and emotions, so the fullness of the Spirit is holistic. When we swallow the Spirit, our entire being is impacted, filled, changed and satisfied with the life of Christ. Swallowing the Spirit forms the life of Christ within, impacting the believer's decisions, activities, emotions, thoughts and relationships.

Functional necessities for swallowing the Spirit

1. Quiet and empty your soul before God by pouring out your heart (Ps. 62:8).

2. Ask God to give his Spirit to you in the name of and according to the work of Christ (Luke 11:13).

3. Commit yourself to swallow the Spirit consistently [keep asking] (Eph. 5:18).

4. Ask for the Spirit when your soul is thirsty, usually several times daily (Eph. 5:18).

5. Specifically ask what you need from the Spirit to form the life of Christ within you (Gal. 2:20). The ask might include fruits of the Spirit, different attitude, Jesus' perspective, other alternatives to consider, transformation of an emotion, perseverance, control of the tongue, etc.

6. Cooperate with the life of Christ being formed in you (Rom. 12:2).

A few miles from where I live is a turn-off from a busy state highway that reminds me of my responsibility in swallowing the Spirit. The turn-off is a small patch of worn grass and dirt some fifty feet off the highway. Next to the turn-off is an old, one inch diameter pipe with water flowing out of it. The water flows into a small tank that sits on the ground. The pipe functions as a relief valve for an underground spring. I suppose the state technically owns it, but everyone is free to stop and help themselves to the water. The water which flows from that pipe is some of the best I've tasted. It is always cool and refreshing with a unique taste, not too strong with minerals but just right! I used to work construction and after long, hot days of heavy work our crew would often pull over by the spring pipe and fill our bodies with spring water. I have fond memories of sitting in the ditch, watching cars go by, relaxing and drinking that refreshing water. Nothing compared with the replenishment that came from that simple pipe of flowing spring water on a hot afternoon.

The water from that spring pipe will never stop flowing. The old timers say it's been there as long as they can remember. It flows 24/7, 365 days a year, every year, and it's free! Anyone can stop and drink from it, fill up multiple containers or drink as much as you can hold as often as you wish. But the most amazing and sad thing about that spring pipe is how few people drink from it. I've asked publicly for a show of hands while preaching sermons in the area. Almost everyone in our area has driven on that road, but only about 20% of people say they've noticed the spring pipe. Of those, only a handful have ever stopped to drink from it. What a tragedy! It's the best water around. Why don't more stop to drink? They are too busy, moving too fast on their journeys to notice it exists. Lives preoccupied with relationships, work, ambition, staying on schedule and the satisfaction of temporal pleasures miss the opportunity to stop and enjoy.

God is a stream, a fountain, a river of living water free to all. He's the best you can find. Anyone can receive water from God, but so few do. All that is needed is to slow down, pull over and stop. Go to the fountain of living water and swallow deeply. Drink whenever your soul thirsts. The water is always flowing, always refreshing, always free and always enough. Take others with you and enjoy it together. It will always be there, flowing along. All you need do is slow down, pull over, stop and swallow.

A friend of mine summarized it this way: "Find the stream of living water and live by it." That is great advice! Stay connected in Christ, empty yourself, ask and swallow. Stay by the stream, live by the river of living water where everything lives, and drink often. Accept the invitation of Revelation 22:17: "The Spirit and the bride say, 'Come!' And let him who hears say, 'Come!' Whoever is thirsty, let him come; and whoever wishes, let him take the free gift of the water of life." What an incredible invitation! The water of life is poured out for us in Christ. It is free and easy to swallow—ask!

In the next chapter, we'll analyze one final activity common to David's psalms – praise. Praise is the delightful dessert of consuming Christ. Satisfaction in Christ is incomplete until it is expressed through praise. This chapter will help you plan to praise, making it a fixed habit of your life. Remember to lay the book down and practice praise.

A Prayer of Swallowing from Andrew Murray

O my Father! There is nothing I desire so much as to be filled with the Holy Spirit. The blessings He brings are so unspeakable. They are just what I need. He fills the heart with Your love and with Yourself. I long for this! He breathes the mind and life of Christ into me, so that I can live as He did, in and for the Father's love. I long for this! He supplies power from heaven for all my walk and work. I long for this! O Father! Please give me the fullness of Your Spirit today. (With Christ in the School of Prayer 58-59)

QUESTIONS FOR THOUGHT AND INTERACTION
Chapter 5

1. Describe the simple process of swallowing.

2. Take a glass of water and put some in your mouth. Notice that it seems natural to swallow. How is this like swallowing the Spirit in your soul? Take another mouthful. Start swallowing and try to stop. What happens?

3. How is asking for the Holy Spirit like swallowing?

4. If it's a natural thing to swallow, what are the obstacles that keep us from swallowing the Spirit continuously?

5. Talk about the idea of "Spirit gravity." How have you experienced this? What questions do you have about it?

6. Read John 15:1-8. What's involved in daily:
   - staying connected to the vine of Christ?

   - emptying your soul?

   - asking to be filled?

7. In what ways are we like the Dead Sea? How does the metaphor of living water flowing into the Dead Sea, described in Ezekiel 47, give hope to your soul?

Chapter 6
Praise

A great meal is not complete without dessert. Fast food is not a great meal, nor is a family restaurant or even a good meal at home, because a great meal is one you don't have to prepare, and secondly, one you don't have to clean up. A great meal is not just meat and potatoes but meat and vegetables uniquely prepared and beautifully presented. It takes hours to eat a great meal because a great meal includes multiple courses, none of which ought be rushed. Each bite of each course should be savored. A great meal is not so much the quantity of the food, although more is generally better, but rather the quality of the food. Delighting in a great meal demands great food, in a great atmosphere, eaten with people you enjoy.

Who really needs dessert after a good meal? No one. Desserts have little nutritional value, they're expensive, they require more time, but a good meal isn't great without dessert. There is something wonderful about slowly eating (one bite every three or four minutes) a rich dessert while enjoying a great cup of coffee. It completes the entire feeding experience. In speaking of the soul, C.S. Lewis said, ". . .praise completes the enjoyment" (*Reflections on the Psalms* 95). Just as a good chocolate dessert after an awesome two hour meal, completes the dining experience, so praise completes the enjoyment and satisfaction of consuming Christ. Without praise, something's missing. My wife is so passionate about rich chocolate dessert that she often says, *"Life is uncertain. Eat dessert first!"* No one wants to miss out on the best part of the feast, so eat dessert! Praise!

Lewis expressed surprise at discovering the natural response of praise to enjoyment: "I had never noticed that all enjoyment spontaneously overflows into praise. We delight to praise what we enjoy because the praise not merely expresses, but completes the enjoyment" (*Reflections on the Psalms* 93). It was through reflecting on the psalms that Lewis noticed what he called, ". . . the most obvious fact about praise . . . All enjoyment spontaneously overflows into praise" (*Reflections on the Psalms* 95). He went on to describe how the world rings with praise. People spontaneously praise whatever they value: favorite poets, music, the weather, actors, sports teams, children, politicians—anything and everything. We love to praise. We naturally and spontaneously praise what we enjoy because the praise not merely expresses, but completes the enjoyment. Commenting on Lewis's thoughts, John Piper said, "We praise what we enjoy because the delight is incomplete until it is expressed in praise. If we were not allowed to speak of what we value, and celebrate what we love, and praise what we admire, our joy would not be full" (*Desiring God* 49).

I attended a Big Ten basketball game some years back expecting to loudly cheer on my alma mater, the Purdue Boilermakers. While living in West Lafayette, Indiana, my family and I attended Purdue basketball games and thoroughly enjoyed cheering with nearly fifteen thousand other crazed fans. It was hard to discern what was more fun, watching the game or yelling together for two hours until we'd nearly lost our voices. After moving out of state we lost the mid-week winter "pick me up" of Purdue hoops in Mackey Arena.

That's probably why I was so excited about a return to Mackey Arena some years after we moved away. Mackey Arena is divided into an upper and a lower section. There is not a bad seat in the house, but the lower section is coveted by every loyal Purdue fan. My two oldest sons, less than ten years old when we lived near Mackey Arena, had vague memories of games in the upper section. As we drove to the game that day, (the boys now teenagers), I was telling them how great this was going to be because a friend had procured tickets for us in the bottom section, third row from the court. In all the years of watching basketball at Purdue I had never been that close to the floor. I tried to help my boys imagine how loud it would be and how awesome it would be to enjoy a game from the third row.

By the time we took our seats, the entire family was pumped to yell and cheer Purdue on to victory. The pre-game hype from the band and the cute cheerleaders being thrown high above our heads by young men who spent a lot of time in the weight room just added to the anticipation. When the players came out for warm-ups, we all felt like we were watching athletic giants. The crowd noise also exceeded expectations. To hear myself scream

107

above the crowd took extra air and intentional effort, but I loved it!

The first five minutes of the game was everything I'd hoped as Purdue quickly built a twenty-five point lead. Within five minutes, the game was essentially over and all fifteen thousand people knew it. It seemed as if everyone stopped cheering. There was still applause and an occasional "way to go," but the wild, intense praise was gone. The game was so lopsided it actually became boring. I sat through the rest of the game bored and frustrated that I had lost a chance to hysterically praise my team for forty minutes. Although I was happy my team had won and played extremely well, my delight was incomplete because I didn't express it through two hours of loud praise.

What is Praise?

Praise is expressing joy and delight. We praise all kinds of things, from dogs, to children's accomplishments, to cars and sports teams. No one has to teach us how to praise, because praise is a natural response of the soul. When something compels us to praise, we cannot remain silent or fail to express it. Think of driving west with someone you love around dusk and witnessing a breathtaking sunset. One or both people will comment on the beautiful sunset because beauty must be praised. It's how we are wired as human beings—we must praise!

Sometimes I tell my wife she looks great because I know it is important for her to hear. That's a good thing to do, but that is not the kind of praise I'm thinking about. The praise I'm talking about is when my wife has dressed for an evening out and I say, *"You look awesome!"* Such praise is a spontaneous response to the object of delight, in this case, my beautiful wife. This kind of praise just has to be expressed. If later during such an evening out, I sink my teeth into the best steak I've ever tasted, I most certainly will tell her about it— *"This is the best steak ever. It's tender and the flavor is something else!"* Spontaneous praise happens when we feast.

Psalm 92:1 says, "It is good to praise the LORD." Praise, in response to feeding on Jesus, is expressing our delight and satisfaction in Christ. "All who seek the Lord will praise Him. Their hearts will rejoice with everlasting joy" (*New Living*

Translation Psalm 22:26b). Notice it's not that those who seek the Lord should, ought or are commanded to praise the Lord, they just WILL! Praise is a natural outflow of a satisfied soul and, as the praise flows, it completes the soul's joy. Without praise, there may be joy, but it is an incomplete joy. Praise consummates our satisfaction and joy in Christ.

Jesus modeled this for us in Luke 10:21a: "At that time Jesus, full of joy in the Holy Spirit, said, 'I praise you, Father, Lord of heaven and earth, because you . . . '" Jesus expressed his joy through praise. As you read on in that passage, Jesus' joy in the Father is unmistakable. Joy in God is greatest when it is expressed. Many things in our world illustrate this. What would the marriage celebration be for the bride and groom if it were not followed by the consummation of love expressed on the wedding night? It would be incomplete! Marriage without the expression of making love and consuming Christ without praise are something less than fullness of joy. John Piper says, "Praise is the summit of satisfaction that comes from living in fellowship with God" (*Desiring God* 53). It is the satisfied "Ahh!" of the soul.

Praise as Spontaneous Delight

The person who feeds on Christ never knows when the soul will break out in praise. There are moments of pure delight in Christ that must be expressed. Years ago, I led an expedition of twenty-five youth to Jackson, Wyoming for a ten-day high adventure camp experience. To keep the price affordable, we journeyed 1500 miles in passenger vans—two full days of travel. As we approached Jackson, near sunset on the second day, the teens were antsy, cranky and smelly (one of my youth workers labeled it "eau de pubescence"). To make matters worse, it started to rain, hiding the mountains we'd waited two days to see. Some of the teens were downright mad, and I was about ready to pull over and give a high decibel attitude adjustment speech. At that moment something happened that created spontaneous praise.

As we drove west, the rain suddenly ceased. The clouds floated east, leaving a clear patch of sky along the rugged, mountainous, western horizon. As the clear sky expanded, someone shouted, "Look!" What followed was the quickest attitude adjustment I've ever experienced with teenagers. To the north was a brilliant full rainbow, looking as if it were growing out of the Teton Mountain Range. We parked the vans along the highway and sat in the wet ditch while all twenty-five of those teens exclaimed praise: "That is awesome!" "I've never seen anything like that!" "Quick, give me a camera!" "Can you believe that!?" "That is so cool!" The experience would not have been complete had no one said or expressed anything. We couldn't drive on without stopping to express praise. Praise is joy expressed, and when joy is expressed, it is made complete. When praise is not expressed, joy is not complete.

I had a similar experience in the Florida Keys some years back, on a motorcycle trip. We spent the night at a beachfront hotel on Grassy Key. Being the earliest riser of our group, I slipped out to the beach with my Bible and coffee for an early morning experience in God's creation. I read a few verses of scripture and then looked across the ocean to the horizon. The wind was brisk that day and the waves quite large. The wind began to annoy me as I struggled to keep the pages of my Bible from tearing and to keep the sand out of my coffee.

Then I noticed the horizon, far out in the ocean, a line created by slightly different hues of blue between sky and ocean. It was a straight line, level and unaffected by the wind and sand blowing against me. As I pondered, it occurred to me that God is like that horizon—always there, stable and unaffected by wind, waves or other things that annoy me. It became a moment of spontaneous praise as I spoke out my joy in the stability of God. I expressed those thoughts of praise in my journal that day, *"I'm sitting on the beach in Grassy Key, Florida. The ocean is vast and the horizon level and long. It is the 'plumb line' of the world. God, You are the plumb line of my life, the center, the focus, the point to which all else relates. I orient my life from You."* That was a significant moment of praise for me, and recounting it right now compelled me again to praise and renewed my joy.

God's creation often compels praise, as does God's word, as it did when I was recently reading the long story of Jacob's life in Genesis Chapters 25 through 50. Because I read the story without thinking of Jacob as a spiritual giant and patriarch of the twelve tribes of Israel, I noticed something—Jacob was a real stinker! He was a deceiver from his youth. He deceived his father in order to get the blessing that rightfully belonged to his older brother. He deceived his father-in-law and wrestled with God. He showed favoritism among his wives and children. In his old age, he was a bitter man full of resentment for many of his own children. Yet, and this is the part that compelled me to praise, God was faithful to Jacob and blessed him. I praised the God who is faithful even to men who make poor choices. God cannot be anything but faithful to those he loves and calls.

God, you are faithful when I am not. Even when I act in selfishness, anger or covetousness you are still faithful to me. I praise you, my faithful God. When I am inattentive to you, God, you never leave me or forsake me. I praise you because you are always present. You created everything, know everything and providentially direct all things according to your good will and purpose. You help the helpless, accept the rejected, provide for the needy, comfort the grieving, care for widows and orphans, free those who are bound and lift up those who are weighed down. You are worthy, my Lord and my God.

I'll always remember the first time I experienced the book of Revelation as a book of worship and praise. It happened during a Sunday morning sermon by a man who later became my mentor in ministry, Dr. Gordon Zimmerman. Dr. Z was preaching on Revelation Chapter 4, which vividly describes images of angelic beings, thrones, thunder clouds, rainbows and a crystal clear glassy expanse. I remember trying to figure out what all that symbolism meant, then Dr. Z said to just enjoy and worship in response to it. He freed me from having to figure it all out and instead compelled me to enjoy beauty and respond to the beautiful God with praise. After the service my face must have expressed my joy because a choir member questioned me saying, *"Did you feel it?"* I had. I had experienced pure praise as an expression of my delight in God.

A similar experience happened years later when I heard Dr. R.C. Sproul preach from Isaiah Chapter 6 on the holiness of God. I had always thought of God as holy but struggled to intellectually describe what that meant. Dr. Sproul helped me appreciate the holiness of God affectively, in my heart, and I was moved to praise. Full understanding is not a prerequisite to praise. Just writing this creates a few goose bumps as I remember that incredible night.

On October 4, 1997, nearly a million men gathered on the Memorial Mall in Washington, D.C. for the "Stand in the Gap" Promise Keepers' event. Our bus arrived early that day so we had a few hours for sightseeing. As my group squeezed our way in to the Lincoln Memorial with several thousand other men, someone started to sing "Amazing Grace." The reverberating sound of hundreds of men singing "Amazing Grace," written by slave trader John Newton, not only memorialized a great president who freed slaves, but also gave praise to God, the divine emancipator. Corporate worship experiences are some of the greatest times of praise for people who consume Christ. Sincere praise in corporate worship is an expression of joy in Christ, a joy that is incomplete until it is expressed. While editing this paragraph about the Lincoln Memorial experience, not only did goose bumps appear, but tears of joy filled my eyes.

I have the ongoing privilege of being led in praise by all four of my children in various corporate worship services. As I follow their lead in those services, my soul is flooded with joy in God's faithfulness to them. Responding to their prompts as worship leaders compels me to praise with a very special consummation of joy. The joy of God's faithfulness to my children in spite of all my parental failures is a joy I must express through praise of Almighty God. I cannot contain such joy, but shout it as praise with tears of delight to the faithful God.

Praise as Willful Commitment

Psalms 42 and 43 describe a kind of anticipated praise that is intentionally pursued even when the heart doesn't feel like praising: "Why are you downcast, O my soul? Why so disturbed within me? Put your hope in God, for I will yet praise him, my Savior and my God" (Ps. 43:5). Praise completes joy, but the psalmist wasn't joyful in Psalms 42 and 43. The writer acknowledged a downcast soul, yet committed himself to praise. But this wasn't praise that came from a heart of joy. Was this some behavioral attempt to feel better? Was the psalmist sticking a happy face on problems that were buried deep within his soul? Was praise motivated by pragmatism or positive thinking? A deeper consideration of Psalm 42 reveals a deeper understanding of praise.

In Psalm 42:6 the psalmist definitively says, "My soul is downcast within me." The next phrase is very interesting, ". . . therefore I will remember you [God]." When the soul was downcast the writer immediately turned his mind (repentance) to God, intentionally pondering God's essence, character and faithfulness. Psalm 42:8 expresses the psalmist's deep thoughts of God, "By day the LORD directs his love, at night his song is with me—a prayer to the God of my life." These pondered thoughts of God nourished the psalmist's downcast soul. In 42:9-10 the psalmist poured out his soul before God: feelings of loneliness and sadness, physical suffering and the taunting of his enemies. The combination of physical discomfort, emotional turmoil and relational conflict caused the downward spiral of the psalmist's soul.

In Psalm 43, the same writer expressed a craving to swallow God's light and truth: "Send forth your light and your truth, let them guide me; let them bring me to your holy mountain, to the place where you dwell" (Ps. 43:3). Then in 43:4 he said, "Then will I go to the altar of God, to God, my joy and my delight. I will praise you with the harp, O God, my God." After pondering the essence and character of God and pouring out his soul, the psalmist knew he would again praise God from a heart of joy— anticipated joy. At the moment, his soul remained downcast. Does this mean we should wait to praise God until we feel better? No, the psalmist knew that someday his soul would again be filled with joy, so he was taking intentional steps to move toward that point. In anticipation of future joy, he praised God in the present. He praised God in downcast times knowing that he would again praise from a heart of joy.

When your soul is downcast, don't wait around until you feel better to start focusing on and praising God. Instead, move toward God, praising him even when your soul is downcast. Ponder God, pour out your emotional pain and disappointment and soul, swallow all God gives you. Praise doesn't have to wait until the heart feels good. Praise doesn't have to be a spontaneous outbreak of joy. Even though praise completes enjoyment, it can be offered from a heart of anticipation as much as a spontaneous expression of joy. Praise can be offered as an intentional, willful act of the soul, even a downcast soul. All praise in this broken world is anticipated praise, because our joy is incomplete until our Lord returns. Only then will our praise and joy be complete.

Research supports that certain intentional behaviors, like smiling, gladden the heart. A positive word lifts the soul and laughter brightens the inmost being. The reason this occurs is that laughter, and even a good smile, release chemicals in the brain called endorphins. Endorphins are the body's natural painkillers and, when released, produce a general sense of well-being—less stress and more joy. C. S. Lewis said, "Praise almost seems to be inner health made audible" (*Reflection on the Psalms* 93). Is it possible that spoken praise of God could alter the soul, creating greater inner health and joy? Can we intentionally praise God and in so doing experience a gladdened heart?

Psalm 92:1 says, "It is good to praise the LORD." Verse 4 of that psalm says, "For you make me glad by your deeds, O LORD." Thinking about God's deeds gladdens the heart and compels praise. In this way praise becomes therapeutic for the soul. Paul E. Billheimer speaks extensively about this therapeutic aspect of praise:

> It is my belief that a massive program of personal and corporate praise could put a large number of psychiatrists out of business and empty many mental institutions. The quintessence of all our mental and nervous disorders is over-occupation with the personal ego; namely, self-centeredness. . . . Here is one of the greatest values of praise: It decentralizes self. The worship and praise of God demands a shift of center from self to God. One cannot praise without relinquishing occupation with self. . . . Praise produces forgetfulness of self—and forgetfulness of self is health. . .There is nothing like praise to dispel self-pity, defensiveness, and hostility. Praise and such domestic vices are totally incompatible. One cannot praise and sulk. Praise and irritation cannot coexist. (Billheimer 117-118)

114

While not everyone would agree with Billheimer's clinical assessment, I do believe this kind of intentional praise compels joy. Not only does joy compel praise, but praise can compel joy! Praise affects the soul and that is, perhaps, its primary purpose.

Commanded to Praise

Does praise affect the essence of God? No. God is complete in himself whether I praise or not. Does God delight in my praise? Yes, he does. Does God need praise to be complete? No, he does not. Does God command us to praise because he is some cosmic ego-maniac? Not at all. Why then are we commanded to praise God? Perhaps God commands us to praise for our own joy and delight in him. Remember, he wired us to be people of praise. Our joy is not complete until we praise; and when we praise, joy is sown in our hearts.

Billheimer states it as follows:

> To be most effective, then, praise must be massive, continuous, a fixed habit, a full-time occupation, a diligently pursued vocation, a total way of life. This principle is emphasized in Psalm 57:7: 'My heart is fixed, O God, my heart is fixed; I will sing and give praise.' This suggests a premeditated and predetermined habit of praise. 'My heart is FIXED.' This kind of praise depends on something more than temporary euphoria. We are told that at the very moment of the writing of this psalm David was a fugitive from the wrath of Saul. His praise was upon principle, not impulse. It was based upon something more than fluctuating circumstances or ephemeral emotional states. It was praise that had penetrated and permeated the warp and woof of his being. It was praise that had become a full-time occupation. (Billheimer 122)

My application of Billheimer's words: Always, always eat dessert! It is the delight of the feast. And, sometimes, eat dessert first. On days when my soul is downcast, I often begin consuming Christ with simple praise. Look out the window and you'll quickly find something that compels praise. Read just a few words of Psalms and you'll soon be praising. Think about your blessings and you'll praise. Start praise by saying: "God, I praise you simply because you exist. God, I praise you because you are here. God, I praise you because I am alive. God, I praise you because you have created. God, I praise you because I feel things, even though today what I feel is not good. God, I praise you because you are worthy of praise. God, I praise you because I'm downcast and I don't know where else to start." Expressions of praise affect the heart for good and set the soul on the path of joy. Learn to turn the negative energy of worry, trouble and fretting into the positive energy of praise.

Psalm 59 is an encouraging example of praising one's way to a more positive perspective. After describing how his enemies oppressed him, David cried out to God saying, "Wake up! See what is happening and help me! O LORD God of Heaven's Armies, the God of Israel, wake up and punish those hostile nations" (*New Living Translation* Ps. 59:4b-5a) David felt as if God were asleep at the wheel, but he still praised God, "But as for me, I will sing about your power. Each morning I will sing with joy about your unfailing love" (*New Living Translation* Ps. 59:16). It is obvious by the end of the psalm that David's heart was encouraged—the power of intentional praise!

Another illustration, from the life of King Jehoshaphat, is described in 2 Chronicles 20. A vast army from a several nation alliance had gathered together to make war against Jehoshaphat. Alarmed, Jehoshaphat inquired of the Lord about how to respond. God's answer came through a prophet, "Do not be afraid or discouraged because of this vast army. For the battle is not yours, but God's" (2 Chron. 20:15b). As his army set out against the enemy, Jehoshaphat ". . .appointed men to sing to the LORD and to praise him for the splendor of his holiness as they went out at the head of the army" (2 Chron. 20:21b). Verses 22-24 describe how the enemy troops turned on and annihilated each another. By the time Jehoshaphat's troops, led by a company of men praising God, came to an overlook, they saw only dead bodies lying in the valley—no one had escaped. The victory was Jehoshaphat's and the only energy dispensed was the energy of praise to God. No fighting energy, just praise. The valley where this took place was later named Beracah, the "Valley of Praise."

Fear of life's battles compels fighting energy, but praise is a higher action than fighting. What would happen to life's battles if we transformed our "fighting energy" into the energy of praise? As in the Valley of Praise, I expect many battles would be over before they started. In most cases, we'd experience the joyous victory that comes from praise without ever having to fight.

How to Praise

Writing in a personal journal is a good way to express praise. Praise doesn't have to be sung or played on an instrument. It doesn't even have to be spoken, although that's the best! It just needs to be expressed to complete the joy of the soul. So, use a journal to write your expressions of praise. Use words, draw pictures or diagrams. Read a good praise psalm (Psalm 144—150) and let it compel you to write your own psalm of praise. Speak your praise out loud. Go out in a wood and shout your praise. Play some praise music and sing with it or write your own song of praise and put it to music. It will be a delight to your soul, the dessert of your feast. Build or create something not as an idol but as an expression of praise.

Consuming is incomplete without dessert - express praise. It has been said that expression deepens impression, certainly true with praise. As we praise God, His life is formed deeper within us. The more the life of God is formed within us the more we will be compelled to praise, and so the cycle goes. The delight of consuming Christ will be ours: "My soul will be satisfied as with the richest of foods [dessert]; With singing lips my mouth will praise you" (Ps. 63:5). Don't forget dessert. Express your joy in Christ through praising and your soul will be satisfied with the richest of foods!

The next chapter will help you organize the activities of consuming Christ into a personalized "feeding" plan. Proper nutritional intake requires planning, recipes and resources. This chapter will help you develop a plan, time and place to consume Christ. Create a customized feeding plan that works for you.

QUESTIONS FOR THOUGHT AND INTERACTION
Chapter 6

1. Share what makes dessert so special. Compare this to what makes the dessert of praise special.

2. Share a time in the last month when you praised something other than God. What compelled you to speak out that praise?

3. Why is joy not complete until it is expressed?

4. What hinders us from fully expressing praise to God?

5. Why is it so difficult to "praise in faith" during rough stretches of life? How do the examples of praising God even when the soul is downcast help you to praise in difficulty?

6. How is a predetermined habit of praise helpful to your soul?

7. Read a psalm of praise, like any of the Psalms from 144 to 150, and let it compel you to write your own psalm of praise.

Chapter 7
A Spiritual Meal: Randomly Putting it Together

Eating a meal is an occasion compelled by hunger that requires food, preparation and commitment to feed. These four essentials for feeding - hunger, food, preparation and commitment - are consistent across culture, geography and ethnicity. Hunger and commitment to feed, by taking food to the mouth, chewing and swallowing, are universal. Although there are large varieties of available foods and cultural practices of feeding, the real diversity is in preparation and presentation. Countless methods of presentation and combinations of foods, spices and methods of preparation abound around the globe. Culinary artists are continually creating new recipes to keep eating a meal fresh and delightful. Presenting common foods in random, fresh ways to create different meals is huge industry and why all of us enjoy eating out.

For some reason, humans need a variety of preparations and presentations to keep us interested in feeding. Sometimes we feel bored with the same food, prepared the same way, and our motivation to eat is hampered by our lethargy. This is not true of any other species. I feed my dog the same amount of the same food in the same bowl at the same place and time every day, once a day, and he never tires of it. Other than an occasional rodent he stumbles into catching, dry food is all my dog eats. He feeds well each day and is quite healthy. He requires no variety of preparation or presentation. Humans require variety to keep us feeding spiritually.

So far we've discussed four components of consuming Christ: **ponder** gospel meat, **pour out** the heart, **petition in** living water of the Spirit and **praise**. These four are essential to a balanced spiritual diet. They are elements of faith by which we receive the broken and poured-out Jesus. If spiritually we were more like dogs than humans, we could feed the same way at the same place and time every day; but most consumers of Christ report inevitable boredom, just as we feel with our nightly supper menu or workplace lunch venues. We need to change it up.

Variety keeps Feeding Fresh

Think about variety in pondering gospel meat, pouring out the heart, petitioning in the Spirit and praising as different methods of presentation that keep consuming Christ fresh and delightful. Creativity and diversity keep us coming back to the table. When you sit down at a table to feed on Jesus, apply the four "P's" randomly and with variety. Most days I start with reading scripture to identify and "chew" on gospel meat. Gospel truth reveals things in my heart that need to be poured out, so I typically float back and forth from pondering gospel and pouring out thoughts, feelings and sin in my heart. But some days my heart is heavy and before even opening the scripture I need to pour out my feelings, confusion, or decisions with which I am wrestling. After a time of pouring out, my soul is ready to feed on Jesus and be filled with his Spirit and ponder his gospel.

As you practice these essentials of consuming Christ, you'll notice that **pondering compels praise** and **pouring out compels petition**. Thinking deeply and intentionally (ponder) about the gospel of Christ often stirs us to praise God. Praise is common after the first bites of delicious meat have been chewed and swallowed amongst friends at a dinner table. We praise what we delight in. If the steak is a high-grade cut of meat uniquely prepared to the eater's preference, praise may follow every bite. Some friends and I shared steak grilled over orange tree wood in Orlando, Florida over ten years ago and when we are together today, we still praise those steaks. The more you ponder the Christ and the gospel, the more you will be compelled to praise Jesus.

You may also notice pouring out the heart compels a passion for the Holy Spirit to fill the soul. Pouring out leaves one empty, vulnerable, needy, craving nourishment and satisfaction. The only food that can fill our emptiness is the Spirit of Jesus. When we swallow his Spirit, he fills us to overflowing, but because the sin nature has yet to be fully crucified, the spiritual bacteria of sin manifests itself by poisoning our spiritual health and development. That is why, as an expression of our trust, (Ps. 62:8), we need to continually pour out the heart to Jesus. There are many ways to pour out, so mix it up. Writing the thoughts, emotions and decisions of my heart to the Lord on paper works for me. Others may prefer verbalizing the heart to God through audible prayers, songs or loud venting. Others may prefer drawing, sketching or expressing oneself through crafts, sculpture, woodworking or other artistic expressions. Some may pour out by reading psalms or other poetry. Expressing the heart to God through silent prayer in quiet solitude is a legitimate method of pouring out. Vary your methods, but after pouring out, be sure to petition in the life of the Spirit. He is living water to your soul that replenishes, nourishes and rejuvenates.

When it comes to spiritual feeding, some prefer consistency; they like formulas. I have a friend who eats the same cereal for breakfast every morning and has done so for decades. If you like formulas or "steps to follow," arrange the four "P's" of spiritual consumption randomly according to your preference. Consistency of method helps many to be consistent feeders. Whether mixing it up or following a pattern, I recommend a consistent time and place. Commit to a consistent time, find a place without interruptions and develop a plan. Then take the time in the place and work the plan. Make sure your meal includes the right food: Jesus and his gospel, the living water of Holy Spirit and the dessert of praise. However you choose to do it, commit to consistent feeding.

Consistent Consumption: Key to Spiritual Health

We cannot live healthy spiritual lives without consistent spiritual feeding. How many people do you know who eat only one meal per week? Yet for thousands of believers, one weekend Church service may be the only spiritual meal they eat in a week. We drink multiple times every day, yet few souls petition the living water of the Spirit beyond their initial experience with Christ. Has the Church become "binge-ers?" Binge eating is not healthy.

John 6:35, "believes," John 6:54, "eats," John 6:57 and 58, "feeds," are all in the present tense. Believing in, eating of, feeding on and consuming Christ are all present, continuous actions. Salvation in Christ is a matter of continuous belief expressed through feeding on Jesus. Faith and repentance are not one-time confessions but ongoing responses of the soul to a gracious God's initiative in Christ. Saving faith, as Jesus taught, is a present and continuous response of the believing heart to the grace of God that is continually poured out. Binge eating is not healthy. The body needs consistent intake of nutrition and the soul needs a consistent influx of the life of Christ. Consistent feeding produces strength, energy, alertness, productivity, health and vitality; but because spiritual hunger is more difficult to recognize than physical, greater intentionality in meal planning is required spiritually.

Everyone has some type of meal plan or at least routine. Some are more specific and elaborate than others, but even more spontaneous eaters have a routine. The exact opposite is true of spiritual feeding; most people do not have a routine. A consistent feeding routine includes many elements: a time, a place and a plan. The key is to **take the time in a place and work the plan**. Routine eventually leads to habit, until consuming Christ becomes as natural as physical eating. It takes time; be patient. Babies feed on demand. Adults feed according to a routine. Both are appropriate in spiritual feeding, but without a plan neither scheduled feeding nor on demand will likely happen.

Have a Time

Time of day is less important than consistency. Some people eat soon after they rise in the morning. My wife rarely eats until she's been up at least an hour and a half, and then she doesn't eat much. Some skip breakfast altogether, while others eat a big breakfast but skip lunch. Every person has a time to eat, and the more consistent those times, the healthier the eater. The time of day is not as important as the consistency of feeding. While ministering in Venezuela, I learned supper is usually eaten late in the evening, about my bedtime. Venezuelans tend to start their day a bit later, take a long siesta lunch and work later in the day. Time of day is insignificant. Consistency is very significant.

Even though time of day is not as important as consistency, Jesus modeled the priority of early morning time in prayer in Mark 1:35. "Very early in the morning, while it was still dark, Jesus . . . prayed." Jesus also modeled praying during the night (Luke 6:12) and late in the day, toward evening (Matt. 14:23). But his rising early to pray, as recorded in Mark 1:35, demonstrated commitment, because Jesus had been up late the prior night healing people and driving out demons. Rising early to pray after dispensing that degree of ministry energy demanded commitment. Starting the day by prayerfully feeding on Jesus may not be a biblical imperative, but it's a really good idea.

While less consistent than my spiritual breakfast, my family and I seek to have gospel conversations around the supper table in the evening. Sometimes these feeding times include friends, young leaders we are mentoring or extended family. Sharing a spiritual meal with others is always fresh and feeds the soul in special ways. I shared a spiritual meal that was very rich with a brother in Christ today. His insight into scripture was like an extra helping of meat to my soul because I did not recognize the things he pondered in the text we read together. His pondering compelled me to pour out and ponder fresh gospel truth. His spiritual insight formed petitions in my heart. We prayed specifically that the Holy Spirit would enable us to recognize the good work God does in us through trials. We petitioned the Spirit's power to embrace God in trials without trying to escape from the trials. Realizing in a fresh way that God forms the life of Christ in me through trials was food for my soul and will empower me to endure the next season of stress I face.

Whatever time you choose, schedule it with intentionality. If we feed on Jesus only when we "have time," our meals will be sporadic and non-existent in busy times. That leads to malnutrition or binge eating at best. The time doesn't have to be the same every day, but without intentionality and commitment to schedule "spiritual meals," weeks and even months may pass without feeding on Jesus.

Have a Place

Jesus prayed in solitude. "Very early in the morning, while it was still dark, Jesus got up, left the house and went off to a solitary place, where he prayed" (Mark 1:35). Matthew 14:23 describes how Jesus dismissed the crowds and then went by himself to pray. And in the garden of Gethsemane, a time of desperate loneliness, Jesus still withdrew by himself to pray, away from his closest friends. It is not surprising that Jesus taught, "When you pray, go into your room, close the door and pray to your Father, who is unseen" (Matt. 6:6). Luke recorded how

Jesus often withdrew to lonely places and prayed (Luke 5:16). Public, corporate prayer is a wonderful thing. Private prayer, better still. It's good to pray with a friend, a disciple, a spouse, children, work associates and parents, but never neglect the place of solitude for feeding on Jesus.

Jesus also modeled variety in his places of prayerful solitude. He prayed on a mountain (Luke 6:12), in a garden (Matt. 26:36), in lonely places (Luke 5:16) and by a lake (Mark 6:46-47). Once again, the kind of place is less important than having a place. I enjoy a variety of places to feed on Jesus just as I enjoy physically eating in different places (dining room table, restaurants, on the deck, picnic in the grass, in the woods). I consume Christ on the front porch, a desk in the attic that overlooks a pond, the dining room table and my very favorite, the deck of a cottage in northern Michigan in a woods that overlooks a beautiful lake. When traveling, I love to feed on Jesus while gazing upon a mountain or from the beach. And what believer cannot worship while looking over the landscape from the top of a summit? Since God reveals himself through creation, feeding on Jesus in creation is a delightful experience.

Some feed on Jesus while walking or even driving. It's important that our feeding on Jesus be our primary motive when walking and not just an add-on while driving. Focus is key. Spiritual feeding requires more intentionality than physical feeding. Eating a cheeseburger while driving is not a great idea, nor is consuming Christ under the same circumstances. There is value in connecting with Christ through music, pondering scripture and petition while driving, but the car should not be one's primary feeding place. The car is a fine place for a snack, but not for a multi-course meal.

Have a Plan

One of the things that most impresses me about Jesus' time on earth was how he accomplished so much in just three years of ministry. Jesus was the master of "planned spontaneity" and of perfect pace. He never seemed rushed, panicked or frenzied. He trained twelve men to change the world in three short years while making atonement for the sins of all people for all time. He stayed on task, understood and focused on the important without being sidetracked by the urgent. He was incredibly faithful to people who came across his path (the ministry of interruptions) without being distracted from his ultimate purpose. I can't preach, play games, keep my lawn mowed and put gas in the car each week without feeling stressed. I plan a lot, but when I fail to meet the deadlines of my own plan, disappointment renders me ineffective in carrying out the very plan I created. I'm in awe of how Jesus lived his life on earth in perfect balance, according to a perfect plan, executed to perfection. Jesus had an ability to hold his plan loosely without losing focus or being ineffective in execution.

There was a time, early in my Christian pilgrimage, when my "feeding on Jesus plan" was written out very specifically so that I could measure progress and award spiritual marker points to myself on some ridiculous sanctified spreadsheet of my own imagination. My cynicism communicates that I don't do that anymore. But like so many who desperately want to be consistent in consuming Christ through intentional spiritual disciplines, the pendulum of my feeding plan swung from anal complexity and self-imposed pressure to unplanned spontaneity. When time became available (almost never) I let the Bible flop open before me and read whatever page appeared. It's kind of like scrounging through a refrigerator full of old leftovers, throwing some in the microwave and eating while watching television.

A good meal requires a good plan, but the plan is never the object, as plans of spiritual disciplines can become. The object of a good meal is delightful nutrition and a well-planned meal of healthy food served at the right time, in the right place, leads to delightful nutrition. Jesus, our Passover lamb, was broken and poured out for our sins that we might feed on him - delightful nutrition! The plan required is not the object but simply our personal means of consistently feeding on Christ. The four activities presented in this book of pondering gospel, pouring out the heart, petitioning the fullness of the Spirit and praising Christ should not be charted, regimented or tracked on a spreadsheet, but enjoyed like courses of a meal. Move back and forth from one activity to another the way you taste meat, then vegetables and then swallow drink.

Customize your plan to be functional for you without making your plan the object of the meal. Some may choose music, online instruction, Bible commentaries, dialogue with others, books and podcasts. All of these methods of presentation can be helpful if what they present is Jesus, broken and poured out (gospel). Chapter 10 includes a list of resources that may be helpful in customizing your feeding plan. Hold your plan loosely, but follow it faithfully. Change it up often. Your feeding plan should be a delight, not a legalistic burden to you. Consult others and learn from their "recipes" and preparation.

Commit to consuming Christ consistently, regardless of the plan you follow or how much variety you choose. A creatively prepared, beautifully presented meal has no nutritional impact if it is not consumed. Following the same plan or varying ways to consume Christ is fine as long as you are committed to feeding. Don't allow time and energy spent on planning, preparation or presentation to hinder your consumption. Preparation and presentation should enhance your feeding, not become an end in themselves. Feeding requires commitment. Sometimes you won't feel like eating spiritually; feed anyway. Other times, your spiritual meal may seem bland, routine and boring. Keep feeding.

Healthy Snacks between Meals

Feeding on demand in response to symptoms of spiritual hunger or thirst can be thought of as having a healthy snack between meals. I keep a jar of peanut butter and a bag of assorted nuts in my office desk. When I need a break, a bit of energy or just a change of pace, I'll pop a couple nuts or spread some peanut butter on a cracker. A high protein snack invigorates and energizes.

Scripture committed to memory can function spiritually like the food stash in my desk. Memorized scripture provides a nutritious truth snack that can be pondered any time. Go to it when you first recognize symptoms of spiritual hunger, such as discouragement, frustration, worry or sadness. God commanded Joshua to "not let this book of the law depart from your mouth; meditate on it day and night, so that you may be careful to do everything written in it. Then you will be prosperous and successful" (Josh. 1:8). Consumers of Christ need to recognize when they are functioning in human strength. Once you recognize that, pause and pour out the humanistic behavior. Then petition the Spirit to fill you with all you need to live out the word and life of Christ forming within you.

The men in one of my discipleship groups have recently been praying for the Spirit to empower us to *pause, pray and respond*. Responding to people and situations in human strength or emotion doesn't work out very well for us. If we can remember to pray before responding, our response will usually be much different, so we are petitioning the Spirit to help us *pause* (before responding to a situation or person), *pray* and then *respond* by the life of Christ that is forming within us. This idea of pause, pray and respond occurred to our group while studying 1 Thessalonians 2:13, "And we also thank God continually because, when you received the word of God, which you heard from us, you accepted it not as the word of men, but as it actually is, the word of God, which is at work in you who believe." Pondering that text, especially the last phrase, compelled the men to pray for the word to be at work in us when facing the challenge of responding under pressure. Remembering to pause, pray and then respond according to the life of Christ at work within is a mid-day bite of spiritual nourishment.

Later in 1 Thessalonians 5:17, Paul commands us to "pray continually." Continuous prayer is like snacking and drinking between meals. It is not complex or hyperspiritual activity reserved for a select few. Prayer without ceasing is simply ongoing conversation with Jesus Christ in every situation. It is a delightful practice that can be nurtured intentionally but, again, over time, becomes quite natural and instinctive. I recommend two resources: *The Practice of the Presence of God* by Brother Lawrence and *Present Perfect* by Gregory A. Boyd. Pondering God, pouring out the heart and petitioning the Spirit can occur spontaneously throughout each and every day through praying continually.

Music is another means of snacking. Gospel music, (not the ever popular southern genre but any music that declares gospel truth), feeds the soul with Christ. There is real spiritual power in music. The psalms are excellent examples. Music that declares the gospel truth of Jesus Christ ministers to the soul. Playing gospel music throughout the day, in the car and around the house, is continual nourishment for the soul.

In addition to David, others in scripture exemplify spiritual feeding. While no consistent method or formula emerges from biblical examples, those who fed on Christ pondered God and his gospel, poured out their hearts to him, petitioned God for favor and praised him. In the following paragraphs we'll consider examples of spiritual feeding from Moses, Hannah, David and other psalmists from the Old Testament as well as the New Testament Church and Jesus himself. Think through these examples of feeding to develop your own "personal presentation" of the broken and poured-out Jesus that most helps you consume Christ. Emulate the specifics of what these characters poured out and the thoughts of God they pondered. Use their phrases of praise to praise God.

Moses

Moses obviously had a unique connection and communication with God, but what interests me is the pattern by which Moses engaged with God. Moses pondered, poured out his soul, petitioned God's presence, praised God and proclaimed God to the nation. Moses often intentionally withdrew from the community to meet with and ponder God. "Now Moses used to take a tent and pitch it outside the camp some distance away. . . . As Moses went into the tent, the pillar of cloud would come down and stay at the entrance, while the Lord spoke with Moses. . . . The Lord would speak to Moses face to face, as a man speaks with his friend" (Ex. 33:7a, 9, 11a). Moses knew that to ponder God it was important to withdraw and seek God in solitude. The most nourishing pondering of God is done in solitude, with intentionality.

I've never heard God speak audibly as he did with Moses (Ex. 33:11), but God wants me to know him even more intimately than Moses. That may sound arrogant, but it's not about me. Remember, Moses and other Old Testament God seekers did not receive what New Testament seekers can receive (Heb. 11:39-40). While God might not "speak to us face to face as a man speaks with his friend," we have something better - the Spirit and mind of Christ (1 Cor. 2:16). The very thoughts and mind of

128

Jesus can dwell in believers as Christ's life forms within us.

Knowing another's mind eliminates relational guesswork and creates intimacy. Jesus prayed something even greater for believers in John 17:20-21, an actual oneness of mind. Audible conversation is great, knowing another's thoughts is better, actual oneness of mind is greater still. In Christ, we have the greater. As we feed on Jesus, he forms his life and mind in us—a far greater thing than speaking with a friend or even knowing another's thoughts.

Moses also poured out his soul to God saying:

> You have been telling me, 'Lead these people,' but you have not let me know whom you will send with me. You have said, 'I know you by name and you have found favor with me.' If you are pleased with me, teach me your ways so I may know you and continue to find favor with you. Remember, that this nation is your people. . . . How will anyone know that you are pleased with me and with your people unless you go with us? What else will distinguish me and your people from all the other people on the face of the earth? (Ex. 33:12-16)

Moses whined a bit as he poured out his anxiety before God. After emptying himself and gaining some reassurance from God, Moses offered up a bold petition in 33:18, "Now show me your glory." God was gracious and allowed Moses a brief glance at the backside of his presence as God quickly moved away. This brief, backward glance at the presence of God so transformed Moses' face that forty days later, when Moses returned to the people from the mountain of God, they were afraid to look at him because the glory of God still reflected from his face.

Pouring out to God compels a craving for more of God; the empty soul longs to be filled. Just like Moses, feeding believers in Christ receive the Spirit of Christ internally, which transforms us with ever increasing glory into the likeness of Christ (2 Cor. 3:18). We can follow Moses' pattern of engagement with God but receive so much more of God because of the gospel. I used to pray as Moses did, for God to "show me his glory." I thought seeing his glory was the ultimate thing God could do for me. But because of the gospel, God wants to form his glory in me by the life of Christ. As I pour out my sinful self and feed on Jesus, the glory of God will overflow from me through the life of Christ that forms within me. Paul died to himself (poured out) so that the life of Christ might be revealed in his body (2 Cor. 4:10).

Hannah was another in the Old Testament who pondered, poured out, petitioned and praised God. Hannah was barren, so she poured out her soul to the Lord (1 Sam. 1:10, 13, 15-16). Hannah specifically petitioned God for a son (1 Sam. 1:11). God responded and allowed Hannah to conceive and give birth. Her response of gratitude to God in 1 Samuel 2:1-10 is a beautiful prayer of pondering the greatness of God and praising him. The overflow of the Spirit in Hannah was the son she conceived and birthed, the great prophet Samuel. Samuel faithfully proclaimed God and anointed the first two kings of Israel, Saul and David, whose psalms are still overflowing in power to us today.

David's psalms are replete with illustrations of these four expressions: ponder, pour out, petition in and praise. Read the following psalms of David and identify each type:

Psalm 143		Psalm 64	
Petition	Psalm 143:1-2	Petition	Psalm 64:1-3
Pour Out	Psalm 143:3-4	Pour Out	Psalm 64:3-6
Ponder	Psalm 143:5	Ponder	Psalm 64:7-9
Praise	Psalm 143:6a	Praise	Psalm 64:10
Petition	Psalm 143:6b-12		

Follow David's example in these psalms. List things within your heart that David's pouring out compels you to pour out. Repeat some of David's praise phrases as your personal expression of praise to Christ. Ask or petition the Spirit to fill you and form the life of Jesus in you.

In Psalms 30 and 31, David moves randomly from one expression to another:

Psalm 30		Psalm 31	
Ponder	Psalm 30:4	Petition	Psalm 31:1-5
Praise	Psalm 30:4	Pour Out	Psalm 31:6
Ponder	Psalm 30:5	Ponder	Psalm 31:7-8

Pour Out	Psalm 30:6-9	Petition	Psalm 31:9a
Petition	Psalm 30:10	Pour Out	Psalm 31:9b-13
Ponder	Psalm 30:11	Ponder	Psalm 31:14-15
Praise	Psalm 30:12	Petition	Psalm 31:16-18
		Ponder	Psalm 31:19-20
		Praise	Psalm 31:21
		Ponder	Psalm 31:21-24

Write personal expressions of David's verses that are particularly relevant to you as an application to your current situation. Flow in and out of the four expressions randomly as the Spirit of Christ compels you. Progress slowly through the expressions, savoring the truth and presence of Jesus as you consume. Identify the four expressions in the following non-Davidic psalms:

Psalm 43

Petition	Psalm 43:1
Ponder	Psalm 43:2a
Pour Out	Psalm 43:2b
Petition	Psalm 43:3
Praise	Psalm 43:4
Pour Out	Psalm 43:5a
Praise	Psalm 43:5b

Psalm 66

Praise	Psalm 66:1-3
Ponder	Psalm 66:5-7
Praise	Psalm 66:8
Ponder	Psalm 67:9-12
Pour out	Psalm 67:13-15
Praise	Psalm 67:16-20

Psalm 71

Petition	Psalm 71:1-4	Petition	Psalm 71:12-13
Praise	Psalm 71:5-8	Praise	Psalm 71:14-18
Petition	Psalm 71:9	Ponder	Psalm 71:19-21
Pour Out	Psalm 71:10-11	Praise	Psalm 71:22-24

I like to mark the four expressions within the psalms according to the following scheme:

Ponder = <u>underlined</u>   Petition in = CAPITALS

Pour out = **bold**   Praise   = *italics*

Identifying when David is pondering, pouring out, petitioning or praising helps me engage personally with the text. Pour out specific, personal needs in David's pour-out sections (**bolded** text), express deep thoughts of God in David's ponder sections (underlined text), petition the Spirit of Christ in David's petition sections (CAPITALIZED text) and quote David's words of praise (*italicized* text). When personalizing psalms or other sections of scripture, be careful not to violate proper principles of interpretation. Hold to a literal, grammatical hermeneutic as you try to affectively engage with the text. Don't force something on the text that the original writer did not intend to say. Accurately interpret each text according to the writer's original intent within the historical context he wrote and then petition the Holy Spirit to illumine that text to your heart. Below is a personalized example I wrote of Psalm 57, which was powerful encouragement to me during a dark season of ministry. A co-pastor in my church fell into moral failure and I was left, along with the congregation, with an incredible mess. I've put {brackets} around the words I added as my personalization of the text.

Psalm 57, personalized
[1]HAVE MERCY ON ME, O GOD, HAVE MERCY ON ME {because I look to no one else but you for help}. I WILL TAKE REFUGE IN THE SHADOW OF YOUR WINGS UNTIL THE DISASTER HAS PASSED. {This is such a mess, my Lord. I cannot see a way out and I'm not sure what to do.} [2]**I cry out to God Most High, to God, who fulfills [his purpose] for me**. {I know you can bring good out of this for me but I cannot see how. I inherited this mess, nothing I did caused it.} [3]He sends from heaven and saves me, rebuking those who hotly pursue me; {Lord, men who should be supporting me are out to get me. These men are speaking slanderously of me. Others have reported to me how they vilify me.} Selah. God sends his love and his faithfulness. [4] **I am in the midst of lions; I lie among ravenous beasts--men whose teeth are spears and arrows, whose tongues are sharp swords**. {They are tearing me apart. My soul feels ripped by the lying tongues. When will this stop? I have no opportunity to defend myself, Lord. They have cut me off and now speak slanderously of me to others.} [5] *Be exalted, O God, above the heavens; let your glory be over all the earth.* [6]**They spread a net for my feet--I was bowed down in distress**. {They want me out of here. They'll do anything to see

132

me go.} **They dug a pit in my path--but they have fallen into it themselves. Selah** *⁷My heart is steadfast, O God, my heart is steadfast;* {I'm trying to hang in, God, as you've asked me. You've not told me much, only to persevere. I WISH YOU'D GIVE ME MORE. I NEED HOPE MY LORD.} *I will sing and make music.* {*As an act of obedience, not feelings, I praise you.*} *⁸Awake, my soul! Awake, harp and lyre! I will awaken the dawn.* {**Lord, it is so dark around me.** *But I will persevere and praise you.* BRING LIGHT TO MY SOUL. IF YOU WANT ME TO PERSEVERE I NEED STRENGTH.} *⁹I will praise you, O Lord, among the nations; I will sing of you among the peoples.* ¹⁰For great is your love, reaching to the heavens; your faithfulness reaches to the skies. {You will be faithful to me throughout this ordeal for you can be nothing else. DEMONSTRATE YOUR FAITHFULNESS, O GOD, TO ME AND EVERYONE WATHCING. You are good and will do goodly. I trust in you and I am saved.} *¹¹Be exalted, O God, above the heavens; let your glory be over all the earth.* {BRING GLORY TO YOURSELF THROUGH THIS, MY LORD. MAY THE PEOPLE PRAISE YOU, MAY ALL THE PEOPLE PRAISE YOU.}

Whatever text of scripture you read, allow it to compel deep thoughts of God to ponder and burdens of your heart to pour out. Empty yourself before your Lord and then petition in the fullness of his presence. Ask the Spirit to fill you with what you need in your particular context. Ask the Lord to pour in what he knows you need and to change you more into his likeness by forming the life of Christ within you. The template below can be followed to engage with the word and Spirit of Christ through the expressions we've discussed in this book. Use this only as a starting point to "set a table" as you prefer.

Consuming Christ

The template below is one way to set the table with the four "P" expressions of consuming Christ. The template is a beginning point, a game plan if you will:

COME TO THE TABLE: *Pray for the word to penetrate and affect your soul as illumined by the Spirit.*
Read a portion of scripture.

PONDER: *Think deeply about God.*

- Write down some thoughts (bites) the passage reveals about God and the gospel.
- Chew on those bites of truth (think deeper) and write down insight you gain.
- How is this truth relevant to you today?

POUR OUT: *Your heart.*

- Write the current thoughts, feelings, decisions, pressure and heat of your soul.
- What thoughts and feelings does the text help you realize about yourself?
- How does the truth you pondered change your perspective? Your feelings? Your thoughts? Your decisions? Your resolve? Your commitment?

PETITION IN THE SPIRIT

- Ask the Spirit what aspect of the life of Christ needs to be formed more in you.
- Write down what you specifically need from the Spirit to form the life of Christ in you.
- Open your heart and ask the Spirit to fill you with Christ's life, attitudes, thoughts, emotions, motivations, perseverance and wisdom.

PRAISE GOD: *Express honor, glory and appreciation to God.*

- Sing or recite a worship song.
- Finish the phrase, God I praise you because you are . . .

We have not yet considered the example of Jesus who, in flesh, applied these very expressions in communication with the Father. The most extensive prayer of Jesus recorded is in John 17. When John's gospel is overlaid with the other gospel accounts, chapter 17 falls in the sequence of Jesus' prayer time in the garden of Gethsemane the night he was arrested. So it is possible Jesus' John 17 prayer was a part of the prayers he offered during his agony in Gethsemane. John 17 and Matthew 26:42-46 reveal Jesus engaging in all four expressions.

John 17:1-5	**Petition**
John 17:6-10	**Ponder God**
John 17:11-19, Matt. 26:38	**Pour out**
John 17:39	**Petition**
John 17:20-24	**Petition for Christ to be**
	formed in believers

Jesus' praise is expressed in the adjectives he used to describe the Father:

John 17:3	**The only true God**
John 17:11	**Holy Father**
John 17:25	**Righteous Father**

Jesus poured out the agony of his soul in the garden. The Father empowered his son in response to Jesus' pouring out because Jesus was able to surrender to the Father's will (Matt. 26:42-46) and go with his arrestors without a fight. When we pour out our souls and petition in the Spirit, we are empowered to live out the Father's will as Christ forms within us, regardless of the adversity around us.

One final example of believers engaging in these four expressions is the early church gathered for prayer in Acts 4:24-31. They began pondering God, "Sovereign Lord, you made the heaven and the earth and the sea, and everything in them. You spoke by the Holy Spirit through the mouth of your servant, our father David . . ." (Acts 4:24b-25). The Church applied Psalm 2 to their current situation as they poured out their stress, "Why do the nations rage and the peoples plot in vain? The kings of the earth [Herod and Pilate for the Church in Acts] take their stand and the rulers gather together against the Lord and against his Anointed One" (Acts 4:25b-26). After pouring out in verses 25-28, they petitioned the Lord for boldness to speak his word. They also prayed for the Lord to work signs and wonders (Acts 4:30) to accompany the gospel they proclaimed. "After they prayed, the place where they were meeting was shaken. And they were all filled with the Holy Spirit and spoke the word of God boldly" (Acts 4:31). They asked for and received the fullness of the Spirit so the gospel of Christ might overflow from them. These examples from Old Testament historical characters, the psalms, Jesus and the New Testament Church establish a pattern for us to follow in consuming Christ. However you choose to randomly "set your table," make sure your presentation includes pondering the gospel revealed in the word, pouring out your soul, petitioning in the living water of Jesus' Spirit and a great dessert of praise. As the life of Christ forms in you, his Spirit of life, love and proclamation of the gospel will overflow from you.

Paul's words in 1 Thessalonians 5:16-18 describe the fruit of consuming Christ: "Be joyful always; pray continually; give thanks in all circumstances, for this is God's will for you in Christ Jesus." We expect God should reveal his will as a specific life plan and path for each of us and, when he doesn't, we assume his will cannot be specifically known; but the above text reveals God's will for us, very specifically and in every circumstance of life: 1) be joyful 2) pray 3) give thanks. Engaging in these three keeps us in the crosshairs of God's will, always. How do we do these three things continually? Consume Christ. As Christ forms his life in us, we will be **joyful, prayerful** and **thankful** - God's will for every believer in Christ.

> *Lord Jesus, I'm hungry for you but my heart struggles to let go of selfish ambition and narcissism, arrogance and pride, influence and power, the temporal pleasure of toys and things money can buy. You know it is hard for me to let go of these things but I know they are junk food and do not nourish the life of Christ in me. Please tear from my heart anything other than you that has become a part of me so you may fill me without competition or rival. Cultivate my heart to grow your life in me. Water me with the living water of your Spirit that I may overflow your gospel of love and glory. Grant me insatiable hunger to feed on you all the days of the life you grant me. Be formed in me as I feed on thee.*

The soul that is fully satisfied in Christ will naturally overflow Christ to others; that's the focus of the next chapter. We call the overflow of the life of Christ from a satisfied believer mission or ministry. Effective ministry for Christ is simply overflow of Christ's life and power through the feeding believer. When we are filled with the life and Spirit of Christ, our lives brim over spilling his life and joy like refreshing rain on a tired and cynical planet.

QUESTIONS FOR THOUGHT AND INTERACTION
Chapter 7

1. Why is variety of method important for consuming Christ?

2. What do you most need to establish consistent spiritual feeding?

3. What are some ways you can "snack spiritually" throughout a day?

4. Choose any two of David's psalms and identify as many of the four "P's" as you can. Then try to express David's heart in your own words.

Chapter 8
Proclamation: The Overflow of Consuming Christ

A predictable outcome of a fantastic restaurant meal is telling others about it - proclamation! Discovering an awesome new restaurant is not something a person keeps to himself. The one who experienced the meal will tell friends, family and even casual acquaintances. Proclamation of a good meal is the overflow of satisfaction. If only the Church were as passionate to proclaim Christ as we are to talk about newly discovered restaurants.

Martin Luther - theologian, pastor, father, husband, author, leader, mentor, professor - was a busy man. Luther was familiar with pressure, pressure greater than most of us will ever experience. Part of that pressure was time pressure, but Luther understood the priority of feeding on Jesus no matter how busy he was. The more he had to do in a day, the more he confessed his need for prayer. Luther is widely quoted as having said, "I have so much to do today that I shall have to spend the first three hours in prayer." Luther understood the key idea of this chapter: Christian ministry and mission are simply an overflow of the life of Christ formed within the believer. Without feeding the formation of the life of Christ within there is little energy, discernment or power for Christian mission. Christ's mission begins through believers as a natural overflow of Christ formed within feeding believers.

The Overflow of the Life of Christ

Jesus promised the woman at the well that drinking living water from Jesus would cause his Spirit to well up within her to eternal life. As the story unfolds in John 4, the spring that welled up in her also overflowed to others. John 4:28-30 says, "then, leaving her water jar, the woman went back to the town and said to the people, 'Come, see a man who told me everything I ever did. Could this be the Christ?' They came out of the town and made their way toward him." From the spring of life welling up in her came an overflow of proclamation to the people in her hometown. Later in the chapter, John records that many of the Samaritans from that town believed in Jesus because of the woman's testimony. The life she received through drinking the living water Jesus gave overflowed to others who also believed. This is how the mission of Christ is authentically propagated. The woman's moral character and historic unrighteousness were of little significance. What mattered then and now in Christian mission is the Spirit of the Lord Jesus Christ overflowing from transformed believers to others.

Jesus taught this in John 7:37-38. "Jesus stood and said in a loud voice, 'If anyone is thirsty, let him come to me and drink. Whoever believes in me, as the scripture has said, streams of living water will flow from within him.' By this he meant the Spirit, whom those who believed in him were later to receive." Drinking in the Spirit of Christ always results in overflow of living water. It is that flow of the Spirit through transformed believers that advances Christian mission. John Stott describes this unique mission of the church with the following words:

> . . . drinking water becomes flowing water. We cannot contain the Spirit we receive. As William Temple wrote, 'No one can possess (or rather be indwelt by) the Spirit of God and keep that Spirit to himself. Where the Spirit is, he flows forth; if there is no flowing force, he is not there.' We must be aware of any claim to the fullness of the Spirit which does not lead to an evangelistic concern and outreach. Moreover, notice the disparity between the water we drink in and the water that flows out. We can drink only small gulps; but as we keep coming, drinking, believing, so by the mighty operation of the Holy Spirit within us, our little sips are multiplied into a mighty confluence of flowing streams: 'rivers of living water' will flow out from within us. This is the spontaneous outflow from Spirit-filled Christians to the blessing of others. But there is no way to ensure a constant inflow and a constant outflow except to keep coming to Jesus and to keep drinking. For the fullness of the Spirit is to be continuously appropriated by faith. (Stott 70-71)

This description of how Christian mission is advanced underscores the necessity of consuming Christ. God's missional modus operandi is to pour his life into receptive, feeding believers to form the life of Christ in them so they can overflow that life, which, in turn, transforms people and culture around them to the glory of God.

Jesus taught this overflow strategy to his disciples by sending them out on short-term mission assignments. In Matthew Chapter 10, he sent them with specific instructions about where to go, what to say, what to do, what to take and not to take, where to stay, and how to respond to resistance. He summarized his instruction to them with one key phrase, "Freely you have received, freely give" (Matt. 10:8b). Jesus was teaching them to trust the Spirit he would pour into them; he was teaching them overflow. Jesus wanted their mission to be totally sourced by the life of Christ they had freely received. He wanted them to freely give from the reservoir he had freely poured into them. Matthew 10:8 is not some symbolic or metaphorical hype about promoting the mission, but the modus operandi for how Christ's mission advances. The overflow of the Spirit of Christ was even to compel their words, "When they arrest you, do not worry about what to say or how to say it. At that time you will be given what to say, for it will not be you speaking, but the Spirit of your Father speaking through you" (Matt. 10:19-20). Every aspect of Christian mission is outflow of the Spirit. Without the inflow of the Spirit that forms Christ in the believer, there is no outflow of Christian mission.

I try to check the source of my missional pursuits by thinking about the question, "If the Holy Spirit abandoned me, would I notice the difference?" My honest response to that question indicates how much the Spirit is flowing through me and how much of what I do under the guise of mission is human effort. "The Spirit gives life: the flesh counts for nothing" (John 6:63a). "Unless the Lord builds the house, the builders labor in vain. Unless the Lord watches over the city, the watchmen stand guard in vain" (Ps. 127:1). "'Not by might nor by power, but by my Spirit,' says the Lord Almighty" (Zech. 4:6b). Christian mission isn't about me, you or any other believer in Christ. It is about the life of Christ that overflows from believers who are feeding on

Christ.

Another place Jesus taught us this is Luke 6:45, "The good man brings good things out of the good stored up in his heart, and the evil man brings evil things out of the evil stored up in his heart. For out of the overflow of his heart his mouth speaks." Christian mission is only possible from a full reservoir of the life of Christ formed within feeding believers. If mission is compelled by anything but the life of Christ overflowing from a feeding believer, it lacks power and authenticity—often doing more damage to the advancement of Christ than good. For God to use us missionally, the life of Christ must be forming within us; and that will not happen without our feeding on the Savior.

Acts 1:4 is a part of Jesus' commission we rarely think about. "Do not leave Jerusalem, but wait for the gift my Father promised, which you have heard me speak about. For John baptized with water, but in a few days you will be baptized with the Holy Spirit." Jesus was warning his disciples not to attempt mission without the Holy Spirit. To do so makes a mess of the gospel because Christ's mission cannot be effectively carried out without Christ's Spirit. It has been said that trying to do the mission of Christ without the Spirit of Christ is like trying to put out the fire of hell with a squirt gun. Mission is overflow of the Spirit.

Paul said to the Romans, "How much more did God's grace and the gift that came by the grace of the one man, Jesus Christ, overflow to the many! May the God of hope fill you with all joy and peace as you trust in him, so that you may overflow with hope by the power of the Holy Spirit" (Rom. 5:15b, 15:13). The goal of Paul's mission to the Romans was not for the life of Christ to be formed in them, but for the life of Christ formed within them to overflow to others by the power of the Holy Spirit. Paul prayed that God would fill them with joy and peace in the Spirit, not just to be full but so they might overflow.

Paul prayed and longed for the same overflow in the Thessalonians. Paul only spent a few weeks with them, (recorded in Acts 17), so he prayed all the more fervently for their faith: "Night and day we pray most earnestly that we may see you again and supply what is lacking in your faith. May the Lord make your love increase and overflow for each other and for everyone else, just as ours does for you" (1 Thess. 3:10,12). The overflow of the Spirit from Paul and his missionary team brought the life and love of Christ to the Thessalonians, and Paul prayed that same life and love would well up in them to overflowing.

The love of Christ, springing forth from the Spirit of Christ, cannot be manufactured by human effort, will or emotion. The love of Christ only flows from the life of Christ through the Spirit of Christ. Until a person is filled with the life and Spirit of Christ, no authentic love of Christ can flow from him. I'm not saying such a person cannot love; he just can't love with the love of Christ. Any love other than the love of Christ will ultimately fail, no matter how strong the intentions. Paul didn't pray they would love, but that they would overflow with Christ's love.

Overflow Empowers Mission

Since Acts 2, the mission of Christ begins when the Spirit of Christ overflows from the people of the Church. Without overflow, what professing believers do springs from human effort and is not Christ's mission, because Christ's mission is not by human might but by his Spirit. When the Spirit of Christ fills feeding believers to overflowing, power is manifest, the power of God that changes everything. Perhaps the best illustration of the life-changing power of the Spirit's fullness and overflow can be seen by comparing the Church prior to receiving the Spirit in Acts 2 to after. A brief study of Acts 1 in contrast to Acts 2 reveals the following about the Church:

Acts 1 Church	Acts 2 Church and Beyond
Emotionally impulsive behavior	Compelled by word and Spirit
Waiting for the Spirit	Received the Spirit
Received explanation of the mission	Empowerment for the mission
Focused on Jesus	Filled with Jesus
Held back	Sent forth
Jesus ascended	Spirit descended
120 in number	3000 in number
Thought about the gospel	Proclaimed the gospel
Organized leadership	Holy Spirit's leadership

Peter, the leader of the Acts Church, is a remarkable personal example of the difference the fullness of the Spirit makes. Prior to being filled with the Holy Spirit, Peter was passionate about Jesus but lacked real missional power. In the gospels, Peter could be described as a naïve, emotionally impulsive, verbal coward. After receiving the Spirit, Peter was transformed internally by the life of Christ and became an influential leader full of biblical understanding, wisdom and verbal courage. The gospel went forth from Peter with power. The before to after difference was the overflowing Spirit of Christ.

What we feed on forms us and flows from us. Healthy feeding results in productive overflow. Unhealthy feeding leads to ineffective overflow. Diet is essential for fitness and productivity. Those who are physically fit usually follow a proper, balanced diet that produces strength and energy. People who do not eat well demonstrate weakness, lethargy and low productivity. This is all too common spiritually within the professing Church. Those who confess Christ but fail to feed on Christ are missionally ineffective because they are not overflowing. Feeding is believing, and until the Church consistently feeds on the life of Christ mission will not overflow from us.

Markers of Spiritual Fitness and Overflow of Christ's Life

Any attitude or behavioral expression that overflows from the life of Christ forming within feeding believers is mission. Mission happens in families, marriages, neighborhoods, schools, hospitals, factories, playing fields and anywhere else the Spirit of Christ overflows to others from feeding believers. There are numerous "markers" described in the New Testament that identify this overflow. Paul mentions four after his instruction to keep on being filled with the Spirit in Ephesians 5:18 - speech, song, gratitude and submission.

1. Everyday Speech

Immediately following the command to "be filled with the Spirit" (Eph. 5:18b), Paul expresses the primary marker of the Spirit's overflow - speech. "Speak to one another" (Eph. 5:19a). David also understood the overflow of the heart through speech, "I proclaim righteousness in the great assembly; I do not seal my lips, as you know, O Lord. I do not hide your righteousness in my heart; I speak of your faithfulness and salvation" (Ps. 40:9-10a). David's speech flowed from a heart compelled by God's righteousness. David understood the power of speech to proclaim the goodness of God or to promote evil.

David's son, Solomon, also understood the power of the tongue as overflow from the heart. Solomon taught about guarding the heart to restrain evil talk in Proverbs 4:23-24, "Above all else, guard your heart, for it is the wellspring of life. Put away perversity from your mouth; keep corrupt talk far from your lips." The heart overflows through the mouth. A heart of evil will speak out perversity and corruption, but a heart full of the Spirit of Christ will speak out the life, love and truth of Christ. Solomon said a wise man's heart guides his mouth (Prov. 16:23) and the words of a man's mouth are deep waters, but a heart full of God's wisdom is a fountain that flows forth like a bubbling brook (Prov. 18:4). Speech that overflows from good within a heart has power to heal (Prov. 15:4) and promote life (Prov. 10:11). Indeed, the tongue holds the power of life and death (Prov. 18:21). Speech has power to destroy life or promote life—missional power.

Jesus taught the same reality, "You brood of vipers, how can you who are evil say anything good? For out of the overflow of the heart the mouth speaks. The good man brings good things out of the good stored up in him, and the evil man brings evil things out of the evil stored up in him" (Matt. 12:34-35). Good speech cannot come from an evil heart. Good speech only comes from good that God pours into the human heart. James reminded us we cannot confuse the two:

> With the tongue we praise our Lord and Father
> and with it we curse men, who have been made in
> God's likeness. Out of the same mouth come
> praise and cursing. My brothers, this should not
> be. Can both fresh and salt water flow from the
> same spring? My brothers, can a fig tree bear
> olives, or a grapevine bear figs? Neither can a salt
> spring produce fresh water. (Jas. 3:9-12)

When Christians speak from any source other than Christ, the overflow of their mouth is evil. The only time our words have

144

positive impact and missional influence is when they overflow from the life of Christ forming within us. This has implications for all relationships of life.

Think about marital stress caused by words that flow from sinful hearts. Paul taught, "Do not let any unwholesome talk come out of your mouths, but only what is helpful for building others up according to their needs, that it may benefit those who listen" (Eph. 4:29). Feeding believer, don't speak from the sinful nature, but from the fountain of Christ's life forming within you. We can build people up with our words (promoting life) or tear them down with our words (promoting death). The key to wholesome speech is not trying harder, but feeding more on Christ. Water does not flow from a dry well or fountain. There is no point in installing a control valve on a pipe where no water flows.

Husbands, do not speak harshly to your wives (Col. 3:19). Men, do not curse, degrade, disrespect or criticize your wives. You do not realize the long-term damage you do when you curse at your wife. You promote death in her when you speak with unrestrained anger and vile words, and you give the devil a foothold in your marriage (Eph. 4:26-27). Stop it, men! "Nor should there be obscenity, foolish talk or coarse joking, which are out of place" (Eph. 5:4a). Men, if salt water and fresh water are flowing from your mouth to your wife, stop it! But that's the problem: most of you have tried to stop. You seem to succeed until you get really angry, then cursing flows out again. Guilt floods the soul, adding regret and disappointment to an already burdened and frustrated heart. Don't just try harder, feed more. Swallow the fullness of the Spirit, feed on Jesus and petition the Holy Spirit to set a guard over your mouth (Ps. 141:3). Pour out the frustration, guilt and disappointment and receive forgiveness from your Lord, broken and poured out as atonement for your sins. Then feed on him and ask the Lord to refresh and rejuvenate you with the fullness of his Spirit.

Matthew 10:8, "Freely you have received, freely give" can also apply to marriage or any relationship. Husbands, freely receive life, respect and love from the Lord Jesus that you may freely give love (Eph. 5:33) to your wife from the overflow of Christ's life forming in you. Wives, freely receive life, love and respect from the Lord Jesus that you may freely give respect (Eph. 5:33) to your husband from the overflow of Christ's life forming in you. Keep feeding on Jesus and swallowing his Spirit. Unless you keep believing, (consuming Christ), what is in your heart will be insufficient to love or respect. How can anyone love a spouse as Christ loved the Church unless Christ is being formed within? We love because he first loved us and poured his love into our hearts.

My wife and I own a third of a modest lake home with two other families. Some years back, the partners decided to move the existing kitchen from the dark, cold basement to the main floor in a week-long project between Christmas and New Year's Day. We started tearing out walls on Monday and worked twelve-plus hour days to complete the project. By Wednesday evening, when the wives were scheduled to arrive, we men had roughed in the new plumbing, completed the necessary electric wiring, installed, finished and painted new drywall and even set the new base cabinets. Our sons announced the ladies' arrival, which compelled the three men to stand beside the new kitchen arrangement, looking toward the door for affirmation from the ladies as soon as they entered the room. Something about men longs for such affirmation from our wives. We crave it. Upon entering, the other two wives raved about how much we men had accomplished in three days. I waited patiently until I heard my wife utter her first words, "You guys didn't install near enough electric outlets above the counter." My male readers just cringed as I did at the time. My heart sank with disappointment and I began to seethe with anger. I'd been married long enough to know venting anger on my wife was ungodly, so I chose the silent treatment instead, for the next four days! My wife kept asking what was wrong and I kept lying and saying, "Nothing."

The day we planned to leave for home, I rose early and sought the Lord through scripture, prayer, pouring out my soul and asking my Lord to help my attitude. As I poured out my soul, the Savior reminded me that I hadn't sought him intentionally all week because we had worked dawn to dusk on the kitchen project. My soul was dry, my reservoir of love nearly depleted. Jesus helped me realize I was looking for satisfaction in the wrong place when I expected my wife to praise our work. My disappointment was the result of unrealistic expectations imposed on her to meet my deepest needs for affirmation. My four day silent treatment toward her was a sinful outflow from a wounded heart.

That morning time of feeding on Jesus and swallowing his Spirit refreshed and rejuvenated my heart with the life of Christ. A couple of hours before we were to leave for home, I was compelled to grab a reciprocating saw and began cutting holes in the back of the base cabinets in order to pull wires for more outlets. By the time we left for home, I had quadrupled the electric outlets above the countertop, and I did it with a joyful spirit, not cynicism of, "That will show her." Overflow. It doesn't happen without consuming Christ. Freely receive from Jesus and freely give to your spouse. No wife can fully meet her husband's needs, nor can any man fully satisfy a woman's needs; God did not create us with the capacity to do so, but God is a fountain of life. When the Spirit of Christ fills us, we will overflow - where the Spirit is, he flows forth; if there is no flowing forth, he is not there.

Relational coercion instead of Spirit overflow, often determines our relational interaction. We long for validation, which fuels unhealthy competition with others in the workplace. Our insecurities fuel attention-seeking behavior as we seek to extract love from friends and family. When others fail to live up to our expectations, we respond to them with coolness, cynicism or criticism. We exalt ourselves and in our arrogance drive people away, fueling the very insecurity that caused us to seek attention from them in the first place. Our arrogance compels us to talk too much or too little, so that our speech becomes all about meeting our own needs at the expense of others. "What causes fights and quarrels among you? Don't they come from your desires that battle within you? You want something but don't get it [affirmation from others]. You kill and covet, but you cannot have what you want. You quarrel and fight. You do not have, because you do not ask God" (Jas. 4:1-2). We do not ask God, the fountain of life. We do not petition the life of Christ. We do not swallow the Holy Spirit.

Sadly, such arrogant, manipulative, angry behavior isn't confined to marriage or the workplace - we also pass it on to our children. "Fathers, do not embitter your children, or they will become discouraged" (Col. 3:21). Harsh and coercive speech embitters our children. When we verbally dominate our children to coerce them to live according to our expectations, we embitter them. I'm not talking about proper expectations of obedience enforced through godly discipline (Heb. 12:5-11), but the use of power that is driven by parental pride, convenience or shame. Proper discipline lovingly administered in obedience to the commands of scripture, is itself an overflow of the life of Christ. Lavish amounts of lovingly administered corrective discipline and consistent, unconditional expressions of love to children from parents flow forth from a heart that has been filled by the Spirit with the love and life of Christ. Parents, consume Christ so that your love may increase and overflow for your children, and everyone else, just as his does for you (1 Thess. 3:12).

The manifesto of Christian communication is speaking the truth in love (Eph. 4:15). This principle, compelled by love that places the needs of others above self, is the gold standard of how to speak for God's glory as an overflow of the Spirit. These same principles (speak the truth in love from a heart of love) motivate evangelistic mission.

Evangelistic Overflow through Proclamation

Peter's amazing sermon in Acts 2 was clearly an overflow of the Spirit as had never happened through him before. Peter was the quintessential expression of the Church prior to Acts 2, but after receiving the Spirit things changed. Where there had been confusion about the scripture, there was now amazing clarity in Peter's mind about Old Testament revelation of the gospel from the prophecy of Joel and the psalms of David. There is no evidence in the gospel accounts prior to the giving of the Spirit that Peter or any of the twelve understood what the Old Testament proclaimed about the Messiah's death and resurrection. After receiving the Spirit, Peter spoke truth with understanding, boldness and love that resulted in three thousand people being added to the Church in one day.

Gospel proclamation by the Spirit, through believers who overflowed with the life of Christ, became the way God's kingdom would advance on earth. The power of living, pouring, overflowing water that brings life and transforms dry desert-like hearts into fruit-bearing landscapes brought understanding to what was happening as the gospel advanced. Rapid, exponential multiplication was a regular occurrence in the church. As internal formation of the life of Christ gained momentum in believers, the overflowing boldness of the Spirit continued to grow and expand the Church.

Acts 4 describes Peter and John being brought before the Jewish rulers, elders and teachers of the law. This was the very group that interrogated Jesus after arresting him in the garden and initiating his crucifixion. It was the group from whom the disciples fled and amongst whom Peter denied knowing his Lord three times. Yet in spite of their power to permanently silence the Apostles, Peter, filled with the Holy Spirit said:

> Rulers and elders of the people! . . . Know this, you and all the people of Israel: It is by the name of Jesus Christ of Nazareth, whom you crucified but whom God raised from the dead, that this man stands before you healed. . . . Salvation is found in no one else, for there is no other name under heaven given to men by which we must be saved (Acts 4:8-12). When they saw the courage of Peter and John and realized that they were unschooled, ordinary men, they were astonished and they took note that these men had been with Jesus. (Acts 4:13)

OVERFLOW! Just weeks before, Peter had fled from this group. Now he boldly proclaimed the gospel. The only difference was the overflow of the Spirit of Christ that now dwelt within him. What Jesus taught him about mission (Matt. 10) and about the work of the Holy Spirit through him (John 14-16) was being fulfilled.

Peter and John then returned to the gathered Church upon their release and reported all that had happened. The Church spontaneously prayed, the prayer itself evidence of the Spirit's overflow and clarity (Acts 4:24-30). Then, after they prayed, "the place where they were meeting was shaken. And they were all filled with the Holy Spirit and spoke the word of God boldly" (Acts 4:31). Because they were filled, they spoke the word boldly

- overflow of the Spirit. They'd been filled on the day of Pentecost, and now they were filled again - evidence of the continuous filling of the Holy Spirit and why Paul commanded believers to keep on being filled in Ephesians 5:18. But how can something already full be filled more?

Think about a sail boat catching enough wind in its sails to propel the boat across water. That sail is full of wind, but if the wind blows stronger, the sail will receive even more wind. Or think of a balloon that appears full. Blow into that balloon and it will likely receive more. John Stott gives an even more helpful metaphor about the continual filling of the Holy Spirit:

> The fullness of the Spirit is intended to be not a static but a developing experience. Let us compare two people. One is a baby, new-born and weighing 7 pounds, who has just begun to breathe; the other is a full-grown man, 6 feet in height . . . Both are fit and healthy; both are breathing properly; and both may be described as 'filled with air.' What, then, is the difference between them? It lies in the capacity of their lungs. Both are 'filled' yet one is more filled than the other because his capacity is so much greater. The same is true of spiritual life and growth. Who will deny that a new-born babe in Christ is filled with the Spirit? . . . A mature and godly Christian of many years' standing is filled with the Spirit also. The difference between them is to be found in what might be called their spiritual lung-capacity, namely; the measure of their believing grasp of God's purpose for them. (Stott 61-62)

Being filled with the Spirit is not a one-time experience, but an ongoing feast of receiving the life of Christ. Feeding and drinking is believing!

Acts 5 records that a number of the apostles were arrested by the Sanhedrin and before being released were flogged and ordered not to speak in the name of Jesus (Acts 5:40). But because of the overflow of the Spirit through them, they proclaimed, "We cannot help speaking about what we have seen and heard" (Acts 4:20) and "they never stopped teaching and proclaiming the good news that Jesus is the Christ" (Acts 5:42b). Where the Spirit is, he flows forth! Even the Pharisee Gamaliel realized this truth from what he spoke to the Sanhedrin in Acts 5:35-39, "But if it [their purpose] is from God, you will not be able to stop these men; you will only find yourselves fighting against God" (Acts 5:39). Where the Spirit is, he flows forth in proclamation!

Acts 8 describes the first widespread outbreak of persecution against the Church. Many in the Church were scattered throughout Judea and Samaria, (Acts 4:1), but because these believers were nourished and filled with the Spirit, they overflowed wherever they went. "Those who had been scattered preached the word wherever they went. Philip went down to a city in Samaria and proclaimed the Christ there" (Acts 8:4-5). Sometime later, Philip encountered an influential official from Ethiopia who was reading the book of Isaiah the prophet in his chariot. "The Spirit told Philip, 'Go to that chariot and stay near it'" (Acts 8:29). The ensuing dialogue, orchestrated by the Holy Spirit, resulted in the Ethiopian's believing and being baptized on the spot by Philip.

We see the Holy Spirit orchestrating evangelistic connections throughout the book of Acts. Evangelism thrives when overflowing believers recognize Spirit-orchestrated, relational connections and initiate gospel conversations in response to Spirit promptings. An influential official, close to the Queen, became an ambassador of the gospel in Ethiopia because Philip recognized and responded to the Spirit's missional initiative through him. Evangelism is fruitful when we follow the relational orchestration of the overflowing Spirit and obey his promptings; but unless we are continually consuming Christ, his Spirit will not overflow from us, nor will we recognize his promptings or initiate gospel conversations in response to the relational connections he has orchestrated. Keep on being filled with the Spirit, feed on Jesus and pray for recognition of Spirit-orchestrated opportunities to proclaim the gospel everywhere you go.

The Spirit orchestrated remarkable relational connections and overflowed gospel through Paul and Barnabas on the first missionary journey. This is not surprising, because the first missionary journey began in response to a Spirit-compelled call. "While they were worshipping the Lord and fasting, the Holy Spirit said, 'Set apart for me Barnabas and Saul for the work to which I have called them'" (Acts 13:2). The Spirit led them to Cyprus, an island in the northeast corner of the Mediterranean Sea. In a town called Paphos, they met a Jewish sorcerer and a false prophet. The typical church planter would never have invited either of these men to be a part of his core team, and yet the Spirit clearly orchestrated connections with these men. The false prophet told his boss, a prominent Roman official or proconsul, about Paul and Barnabas, so the proconsul sent for them because he wanted to hear the word of God from them. The sorcerer tried to turn the proconsul from the faith, so Paul, "filled with the Holy Spirit, looked straight at Elymas (the sorcerer) and said, 'You are a child of the devil and an enemy of everything that is right! . . . Now the hand of the Lord is against you. You are going to be blind, and for a time you will be unable to see the light of the sun'" (Acts 13:9b-11). When the Roman proconsul saw the sorcerer go blind from the overflow of the Spirit through Paul, he believed. Once again, Spirit orchestration led a prominent official to believe the gospel.

Effective evangelistic effort, whether person to person or church planting nationally and internationally, is the overflow of proclamation within contexts the Spirit has orchestrated. Henry Blackaby, who wrote *Experiencing God*, would likely describe this process by saying, "Find out where God is working and join him" (Blackaby 26). Ineffective evangelism results when we initiate and expect the Spirit to support our ambition.

One of the first intentional gospel conversations I initiated as a new believer taught me this profound truth in a very awkward way. I had been trained in a specific method of sharing the gospel and felt pressure to present it to a friend with whom I'd had very little contact for the past year. I called my friend Don and invited him to lunch at my apartment. (I had never invited Don for lunch anywhere, and he had never been in my apartment). After lunch, I started my presentation. Don listened, but was not overly responsive. I only asked Don for feedback once, and that was at the end of my presentation, after saying something about the gospel needing to be personally accepted. I

152

was ready to "set the hook," so I said to Don, "What about you?" After at least a minute of awkward silence, (I'd been trained to wait out my subject), Don replied, "Humph, what about me?" He then stood up, walked to my door and left without either of us saying another word. My proclamation to Don was all about me, my ambition and my need to feel I was being an effective Christian. Several things were wrong about my approach: 1) It was motivated by selfishness, not love. 2) It was my initiative, not the Spirit's. 3) It was my words and not an overflow of the Spirit through me.

We need to consume Christ and let the Spirit naturally overflow through us, proclaiming the gospel wherever we go. This is how the gospel was effectively propagated through Paul's missionary journeys. The following references in Acts all describe the natural overflow of gospel proclamation wherever Paul went in contexts orchestrated by the Holy Spirit: Acts 13:44, 46, 49; 14:3, 7, 21, 25; 16:32; 17:18; 22:1-21; 23:1-11; 24:10-21, 24-26; 26:1-27. The last words of Paul's gospel presentation (Acts 26) to Agrippa, an opportunity clearly orchestrated by the Holy Spirit, confronted the King with the personal reality of the gospel. Agrippa replied, "Do you think that in such a short time you can persuade me to be a Christian?" (Acts 26:28). I wonder if he ever did.

Gospel proclamation before kings is what Jesus trained and prepared his disciples to do. Without the Spirit it would have been totally ineffective, but the two working together created a powerful synergism. Mark recorded that "the disciples went out and preached everywhere, and the Lord worked with them and confirmed his word by the signs that accompanied it" (Mark 16:20). The word translated "worked with" is a form of our word synergism. Believers proclaimed the gospel by the Spirit's overflow and then the Lord confirmed HIS word by signs that accompanied it. The Acts Church prayed for this powerful synergism of their proclamation and the Spirit's confirmation when they prayed, "Stretch out your hand and perform miraculous signs and wonders through the name of your holy servant Jesus" (Acts 4:30). Our mission, Church, is to proclaim the gospel as an overflow of Christ's life within us and then pray for the Spirit to work his word in others (1 Thess. 2:13). We are

153

to do this naturally, wherever we go.   As the people of the Church initiate gospel conversations, asking Jesus to work his word with synergistic signs in others, the gospel will advance by the power of the Holy Spirit.

Gospel proclamation as a natural overflow of the Spirit from a nourished believer in Christ should be normal Christian behavior. The Great Commission of Jesus "makes disciple-making the normal agenda and priority of every church and every Christian disciple . . ." (Marshall 13) ". . . proclaiming (speaking the word) and praying (calling upon God to pour out his Spirit to make the word effective in people's hearts)" (Marshall 41). Overflow of gospel proclamation should happen consistently in evangelistic contexts and all venues because the "go" in the commission could be accurately translated "as you go" or "wherever you go."   How can the life of Christ flow from us if we are spiritually malnourished, dry and empty?   "Where the Spirit is, he flows forth; if there is no flowing forth, he is not there" (Stott, 70). There will be no overflow of "speaking to one another" (Eph. 5:19a) unless we consume Christ. In Ephesians 5, Paul teaches the Spirit will overflow in ways additional to natural, daily conversation.

2. Song

After commanding believers to keep on being filled with the Spirit in Ephesians 5:18, Paul taught we should sing as an overflow of the Spirit. "Sing and make music in your heart to the Lord" (Eph. 5:19b).   Music is a wonderful gift of God and another venue for Spirit overflow.   Singing is another natural overflow of a satisfied soul. "My soul will be satisfied as with the richest of foods; with singing lips my mouth will praise you" (Ps. 63:5). Joy is perhaps best expressed through song. Music is part of most joyous events in almost every culture—weddings, parties, sports and ceremonies of all kinds. Paul hoped the Philippians' joy in Christ would overflow when he was with them (Phil. 1:26) and Peter taught that the fullness of joy in Christ is so glorious that it cannot be adequately expressed (1 Pet.1:8). Music allows us to express the affective dimension of the life of Christ within us. Pondering Jesus naturally overflows into worship and praise of the one we ponder. Worship is focusing on God and then responding to him. Responding to God is an overflow of joy that comes from focusing on or pondering God's essence, character and righteous deeds. John Piper says, "Love is an overflow of JOY in God which meets the needs of others" ("Love. . ." *desiringGod*) and what is a more prominent theme in music than love?

Another overflow of the Spirit that can be expressed through song is hope, "May the God of hope fill you with all joy and peace as you trust in him, so that you may overflow with hope by the power of the Holy Spirit" (Rom. 15:13). Great worship songs express hope. Stories of overflowing believers singing as they were martyred for their faith express supernatural hope. Paul and Silas sang hymns from prison while their feet were shackled in the stocks, an overflow of their hope in the Lord. Hope, when used in the New Testament, means a confident expectation in the Lord, not a wish list of personal favors we impose on the Lord. Overflowing confidence in the Lord (hope) empowers bold endeavors but also inspires everyday initiative. Living by hope or confidence in Christ is what Brother Lawrence expressed in his classic writings *The Practice of the Presence of God.*

3. Gratitude

A third overflow of Spirit fullness Paul mentions in Ephesians 5:20 is gratitude, "always giving thanks to God the father." In 2 Corinthians 4:15, Paul reminds the Corinthians of the benefits of the gospel and how it causes "thanksgiving to overflow to the glory of God." Gratitude is another natural outflow of the Spirit formed within the heart of believers. Paul encouraged believers in Thessalonica to give thanks in all circumstances (1 Thess. 5:18). Gratitude in ALL circumstances has great missional power because others most notice our thankfulness when we are enduring hard times. When people around us SEE us struggling but HEAR our gratitude in the midst of the struggle, they wonder how we do it. We don't do it, but the Spirit flowing through us does.

God will use personal trials in a missional way to overflow comfort to others. "Praise be to the God and Father of our Lord Jesus Christ, the Father of compassion and the God of all comfort, who comforts us in all our troubles, so that we can comfort those in any trouble with the comfort we ourselves have received from God. For just as the sufferings of Christ flow over into our lives, so also through Christ our comfort overflows" (2 Cor. 1:3-5). This sense of "purpose in pain" empowers gratitude and perseverance to the glory of God. The Spirit assures that even trouble, although not necessarily caused by God, is God's servant. The cross of Christ is the greatest example of this reality. In one sense, the crucifixion of Jesus was the most despicable, heinous act of human evil ever perpetrated, but God redeemed the evil against his son to appease his own wrath against human sin and buy his people back from the clutches of evil. God can redeem the most heinous, wicked evil for the most glorious good.

"Out of the most severe trial, their overflowing joy and their extreme poverty welled up in rich generosity" (2 Cor. 8:2). Generosity is another overflow of gratitude from the fullness of the Spirit. The Thessalonians lived in extreme poverty, and yet generosity welled up within and flowed from them:

> This service that you perform is not only supplying the needs of God's people but is also overflowing in many expressions of thanks to God. Because of the service by which you have proved yourselves, men will praise God for the obedience that accompanies your confession of the gospel of Christ, and for your generosity in sharing with them and with everyone else.
> (2 Cor. 9:12-13)

Overflowing Thessalonian generosity not only provided for others but also compelled gratitude and praise to God from others.

4. Submission

Finally, in Ephesians 5:21, being continually filled with the Spirit compels mutual submission. Godly relational submission is key evidence of the fullness of the Spirit because submission is not a natural outflow of sinful, human nature. The default setting of our sin nature demands our own way contrary to submission. Perhaps Paul follows this command with the most extensive instruction on marriage in the scripture because submission is so very difficult in the marriage relationship. Christ-centered marriage is an overflow of the Spirit's fullness where husband and wife submit to one another within their unique roles and function as Paul describes in Ephesians 5:33, "each one of you also must love his wife as he loves himself, and the wife must respect her husband."

Romans 8 describes submission with compulsions common to marriage—desire and control. We want control, but submission to the Spirit requires a surrender of control.

> Those who live according to the sinful nature have their minds set on what that nature desires; but those who live in accordance with the Spirit have their minds set on what the Spirit desires. The mind of sinful man is death, but the mind controlled by the Spirit is life and peace; the sinful mind is hostile to God. . . . Those controlled by the sinful nature cannot please God. You, however, are controlled not by the sinful nature but by the Spirit, if the Spirit of Christ lives in you. And if anyone does not have the Spirit of Christ, he does not belong to Christ. (Rom. 8:5-9)

"If the Spirit of Christ lives in you" - that's the key to being controlled by the Spirit. Where the Spirit is, he flows, he controls. Once the life of Christ exists within the soul, by the power of the Spirit mutual submission naturally occurs.

The overflow described in this chapter is a small sampling of the numerous ways the overflow of the Spirit is taught, illustrated and encouraged in the scripture. Authentic Christian life, ministry and mission are an overflow of the Spirit, but there are things that hinder the overflow. These "overflow restrictors" are also numerous, but many fall into one of three categories: narcissism, hypocrisy and dryness.

OVERFLOW RESTRICTORS

The sin nature works against the indwelling Spirit (Romans 7:14-25) so the believer must be aware of how and surrender those specifics to the Lordship of Christ.

1. Narcissism: Full of Self and not the Spirit

A number of years ago, a parishioner in our congregation gave my wife and me a once in a lifetime, week-long trip to a resort in Maui. It was the most refreshing vacation we had ever experienced. There was no one on Maui who needed our attention, no telephone ringing, no schedule or deadlines to meet, no hurry or busyness, just rest and relaxation. The most stressful thing we engaged in that week was a luau on the beach with scores of other vacationers. We sat across the table from a delightful young couple from Australia. A couple of times throughout the evening I sensed the Spirit nudging me to engage the couple in a gospel conversation. I floated a few quasi-spiritual comments, but the couple didn't respond. I remember thinking to myself, "Oh, well, I'm on vacation," as if the overflow of the Spirit only happens through me when I'm "on the clock" as a pastor. My attitude was indicative of the vacation I had taken from feeding on Christ while in Hawaii, so my heart, instead of overflowing with gospel proclamation, was dry and lazy - selfish stubbornness that refused to obey the Spirit's prompting. I didn't realize the restricted flow of the Spirit in me until hours later. By then I longed to see the couple again to have another go at a gospel conversation, but I never saw them again. That was at least fifteen years ago, and the missed opportunity still haunts me today. I pray I will see them in heaven someday because of someone else's faithfulness of proclaiming the gospel. Where there is no fullness of the Spirit, there is no overflow.

2. Hypocrisy: Proclamation without Fruit

The Spirit uses fruit to multiply the gospel. Hypocrisy, proclaiming the gospel without demonstrating the fruit of the gospel, destroys multiplication. Without fruit there is no multiplication because the seeds of the fruit are what causes new birth in others. Believers proclaiming gospel without seeds of gospel fruit flowing from their lives hinder the spread of the gospel. Proclamation without fruit is hypocrisy, but fruit without proclamation is disobedience.

I took a ten day break from writing this book because of two out-of-town weddings on consecutive weekends and a short golf trip squeezed in between the weddings. Our children, grandchildren and some informally adopted children of ours all stayed in three hotel rooms on the weekend of the second wedding. We were all together for three days. In the chaos of being away from home and living with multiple people, I failed to intentionally "feed on Jesus" for three days. While driving home from the wedding, I felt sad, lonely, (my wife was asleep in the car as always on trips), grouchy, frustrated and anxious about the week ahead. It had been a great and joyous week. So why was my soul downcast? I wasn't tired, sore, injured, sick or worn out physically, but I felt that way spiritually.

When I rose early the next morning to feed on Jesus for the first time in four days, I was spiritually hungry, even malnourished. I had allowed busyness and change of routine to keep me from consuming Christ. I felt fine physically because I had been eating well. I took advantage of the hotel breakfast buffet every morning, had nice lunches and wonderful evening meals. I also sampled plenty of snacks from our hotel room throughout the days. Had I fed spiritually with the same zeal and consistency, my soul would have been in a much different place, but my soul was malnourished. I had failed to abide in the vine of Christ for three days, so the flow of the Spirit's life was restricted in me. Fruit does not grow when the branch is not abiding in the vine. Fruit requires consistent connection to feeding on the life of Christ.

This important instruction of Jesus in John 15:1-8 teaches that fruit is an organic by-product of sap from the vine flowing to and through a branch that stays connected to and feeds on sap from the vine. Believers are branches through whom the sap that creates the fruit flows. The only thing required of the branch, from Jesus' instruction in John 15, is to remain connected to him, the vine. The believer's responsibility in bearing fruit is passive, because it is the Spirit (or nourishing sap from the vine) that grows fruit in us. "No branch can bear fruit by itself; it must remain in the vine" (John 15:4).

Fruit develops over time; it is not instantaneous. Human effort does little to change the timeline; a branch cannot hurry the flow of the sap. Discouragement in the short term gives way to obvious and unmistakable fruit after a season of growth. We may not be able to accelerate the growth of the fruits of the

Spirit, but we can hinder fruit development by failing to abide in and feed on the sap of the Spirit. God cuts off branches that fail to produce fruit and prunes other branches to produce more fruit (John 15:2). This is a harsh reality of God's order in Christ. Believers will bear fruit. That is how believers are recognized, according to Jesus: "By their fruits you will recognize them" (Matt. 7:16). When a healthy branch is connected to a healthy, growing vine, there will be fruit; it cannot be stopped. Connected branches that continue consuming Christ will bear fruit exponentially.

Paul's description of the fruit of love in 1 Corinthians 13:4-8a is a significant gauge, "Love is patient, love is kind. It does not envy, it does not boast, it is not proud. It is not rude, it is not self-seeking, it is not easily angered, it keeps no record of wrongs. Love does not delight in evil but rejoices with the truth. It always protects, always trusts, always hopes, always perseveres. Love never fails." These characteristics help us recognize the fruit of love; and recognizing the development of fruit, whether love or the other fruits, is evidence of spiritual health and vitality which comes from the Spirit as we feed on Jesus.

Fruits of the Spirit develop organically as the Spirit determines, but feeding on Jesus is necessary for fruit development, because those who do not feed on Jesus have no life (fullness of the Spirit) in them (John 6:53). It's not that our feeding produces fruit, but unless we feed (as a branch draws sap from the vine), fruit won't develop because the Spirit won't be flowing to and through us. Fruit development in the life of a feeding believer is about cooperation with the flow of the Spirit to and through us.

Our responsibility is like that of a fruit farmer, who cannot produce fruit by human effort but can create conditions favorable for development of fruit. A farmer's actions are dictated by weather. Corn farmers in our area do not plant corn in January because conditions are not right for growing. They don't plant when it is too wet or wait until too late in the growing season when it's dry. When the time is right and the weather conditions are favorable, the farmer prepares the soil to receive seed. The weather and the soil conditions dictate the farmer's behavioral choices. Instead of trying to control rainfall, the farmer does his best to cooperate with it. He plans all his farming activities in cooperation with anticipated rainfall. We cannot control the flow of living water, but as we do our best to cooperate with the expected filling of the Spirit, good fruit will grow over time.

It is essential to cooperate with Jesus being formed in us. What do we need from Jesus to develop fruit? The Spirit of living water. What does Jesus need from us to develop fruit? Our cooperation and organic connection to him. Jesus is not stingy with the flow of His Spirit, so if the flow of the Spirit is restricted to and through us, it is due to a lack of cooperation. So how do we cooperate with the life of Christ working in us to bear fruit?

I heard my mother say countless times of me while I was growing up, "There is not a gentle bone in his body." In my early years of marriage, my wife often said, "Be gentle." Even a gruff construction friend I worked with used to say to me, "Easy, gentle now." Gentleness is not innate in me, not even a little. As I grew more intentionally cooperative about the life of Christ forming in me, I worried about the lack of gentleness fruit in me. I made some behavioral adjustments, like slowing down and quieting myself, but nothing seemed to make me significantly more gentle.

About thirty years ago, I decided to seriously investigate what the Bible says about gentleness. I made a schedule and read several verses on gentleness each day while on vacation for a week. I memorized a few of the key summary verses. Philippians 4:5 stuck out to me and reflected what I desired, "Let your gentleness be evident to all. The Lord is near." Following vacation, I began to pray daily for that verse to become reality in my life. I truly desired the Spirit to develop gentleness in me, as did my wife, mother and everyone else around me. Three decades later, I confess with authenticity, I am more gentle than I used to be and it's not just because I'm older. Three decades seems like a long growing season, but I have experienced the Spirit slowly but steadily growing that fruit in me. I recognize it in my marriage, with my children and even with men in small groups or at men's retreats.

I did not make that fruit grow; I just intentionally cooperated with the Spirit's flow by petitioning the life of Christ to specifically form gentleness in me. I desired gentleness, acknowledged my dependence on the Spirit for it and petitioned the Lord Jesus to grow it as part of his life forming in me. I was a passive recipient, a branch clinging to the vine, a receiver of life-creating sap. I cooperated with what Jesus wanted to develop in me by desiring and praying for it to occur. I couldn't see the development of the fruit from day to day, but it's there now.

As I write from my third floor desk overlooking the backyard of our country home, I see the first few annoying dandelions of spring growing within a few feet of our pond. They receive plenty of moisture there, which is enabling them to grow more quickly than the dandelions anywhere else in the yard. I see ten to twelve well-nourished yellow flowers that will multiply into thousands within a number of weeks if I don't intervene. The fruit of those yellow flowers (seeds) will be blown by the wind and take root throughout my yard.

Jesus taught in the parable of the sower that the word of the gospel is like those seeds. Fruit of the life of Christ forming in believers produces seeds of gospel that believers can proclaim to others. Proclamation sows the seeds, but without fruit there are no authentic seeds to sow. The whole process is governed by the wind, water and growing power of the Holy Spirit. Oh, that the church of Jesus would multiply like dandelions! Oh, that the wind of the Spirit would blow the fruitful overflow of the life of Christ from believers as dandelions seeds are scattered. It only takes a few fruitful flowers to grow thousands of plants.

3. Spiritual Dehydration: Greater Outflow than Inflow

Intense ministry outflow, if not sourced by inflow of the Spirit, can cause spiritual dryness. All ministers of the gospel are vulnerable, because those who give and give without the diligence to receive the invigorating life of Christ and refreshment of his Spirit can become dry rather quickly. This is a dangerous condition for the Church.

I had only been a senior pastor for a couple of years when I learned the need to take in more of the Spirit than was overflowing from me. My aged grandfather, who lived in the same county as the Church I ministered in, was dying of congestive heart failure. My wife and I had spent a significant portion of every day that week by his bedside, praying, reading scripture and singing hymns to him. That Saturday, I hit the bed early to gain much needed rest for preaching two services in the morning. About midnight, the phone rang and a parishioner summoned me to the same CCU ward where I had spent hours that week with my grandfather. The parishioner's father, whom I'd visited several times that week, had taken a bad turn and was in his last hours. This only son asked me to sit with him by his father's bedside until he passed. We prayed, read scripture and sang at his bedside until he passed about 5:30 am. I prayed a final time with the surviving son and went home to shower before heading immediately to Church to preach two services and teach a Sunday School class.

Following Sunday services, I stopped by to see Grandfather in the same CCU where I had spent the night praying. After a brief visit, I walked through the waiting room and was apprehended by a parishioner there. The woman told me about a frustrated friend of hers, another parishioner of mine, who desired some of my time. The waiting room visitor said in a sharp, demanding tone, "Marie is upset that you haven't been to see her in a long time." Those harsh words stuck to me because I was empty and exhausted, with no emotional or physical energy left to give. I realized in that moment that I would never have enough energy or time to meet the expectations or demands of pastoral ministry. I simply did not have the capacity to give enough. That sharp rebuke stuck to me and I ministered with resentment for months.

But as the Spirit filled and refilled me, he brought healing. As the life of Christ formed more within me, he taught me something about ministry—I do not have what it takes. I never will; I can't do it. Ministry is the overflow of the Spirit through me, not more of my human energy and not trying harder to please people. I began to consume Christ and swallow the Spirit as never before. Ever since, I've been able to recognize spiritual dryness a bit more easily and can go back to the well of life before I'm so dry that everything negative sticks to me. I've also learned that when the Spirit is overflowing from me, nothing really sticks to me.

Picture a container connected to a water source so water that is flowing to the container is pressurized. Imagine the container is full, but water is still flowing under pressure to the container. This will produce overflow, significant overflow. Now throw something sticky at the container. What happens? Nothing, absolutely nothing. The sticky lump doesn't stick to the container because the flowing water won't allow it. This revolutionized my ministry. If I am full of Christ to overflowing every day, nothing negative will stick to me! Holy Spirit overflow that keeps the negative, harsh, critical "stickys" from sticking is an incredible experience.

This is true in all relationships, not just in pastoral ministry. People say and do negative, hurtful things in relationships that stick to our hearts. These create pain, anger, resentment and bitterness if not resolved. The best antidote to these negative responses is to guard oneself from the negativity sticking to the heart in the first place. Negative expressions don't stick to a heart that is overflowing with the life and love of Christ by the power of the Spirit. God's will for believers is to be joyful always, praying continually, and to be grateful in all circumstances (1 Thess. 5:16-18), all of which are an overflow of the Spirit. These three, joy, prayer and gratitude, insulate our hearts from things sticking to us. The overflow of joy, prayer and gratitude allows us to consider it pure joy whenever we face trials.

The wife of an immoral husband can still overflow love and commitment to that adulterer while remaining joyful and grateful even though she has been terrible betrayed. His adultery need not stick to her heart. The employee unjustly passed over for a promotion can pour out disappointment, petition in the fullness of the Spirit and still overflow with thankfulness for his job while working faithfully for the very employer who disappointed him. The lonely person who consumes Christ can enjoy sweet oneness with him without the stickiness of loneliness. Even those who have been wronged unjustly, or even heinously, can be filled with the Spirit of Jesus to overflowing and free from the "stick" of injustice.

Jesus said in John 10:10b, "I have come that they may have life and have it to the full." The word "full" expresses a Greek idea which means "superabundant or excessive;" in other words, overflowing. Jesus came not just to save you from your sins, not just to fix your problems, not just to make God known to you, not just to make you a "better" person, but he came to give you life, his life – abundant and overflowing. A form of the same word is used in Ephesians 3:20, "Now to him who is able to do immeasurably more than all we ask or imagine. . . ." "Immeasurably" is a translation of two Greek words which the King James version translates as "exceeding, abundantly above." The idea is God can do above, above what we can even imagine. He is able to fill us to overflowing and then overflow that overflow. Your savior is able to fill you to overflowing with his life. He is able to form his life in you so that you no longer live but he lives in and overflows from you. But you must want him, you must feed on him, you must swallow his Spirit and consume him who was broken and poured out for you. "Let us cry out to our Father to so fill us with Spirit that our lives brim over, spilling His life and joy like refreshing rain on a tired and cynical planet" (Lewis and Demarest Vol III 215).

This book began with an illustration of hunger from my dear friend Mary. Mary was deceived by dementia into thinking she was always hungry. We are often deceived by the world into thinking we can satisfy the need of our souls through feeding on things other than Jesus Christ. The final chapter will help us recognize our spiritual hunger and need to feed on Jesus.

QUESTIONS FOR THOUGHT AND INTERACTION
Chapter 8

1. Why do we so infrequently proclaim Jesus to others if overflow is a natural outcome of a soul satisfied in Christ?

2. What is some evidence of overflow from a believer's life?

3. What most restricts overflow of the life of Christ from your soul?

4. How can you more effectively cooperate with the Spirit who forms the life of Christ in you?

5. What can you do this week to avoid spiritual dehydration?

Chapter 9
Recognize the Need to Feed: Avoiding Malnutrition and Dehydration

God designed living things with a remarkable ability to recognize when the body needs nourishment. It's simple and universal to all animals - hunger. Hunger is the primary motivation of animals in the wild most hours of any day. The need to feed is primary, so animals are driven to find food. Without food and water, no animal lives more than days or weeks. Hunger compels feeding and feeding promotes life, keeping us healthy, vital and strong.

Recognizing the need to feed spiritually sometimes requires a bit more intentionality. Spiritual hunger may be more difficult to recognize, but parallels to physical hunger can help us identify our need to feed spiritually. Prominent symptoms of hunger include: cravings, emptiness, weakness, lethargy, fatigue, obsession with food, (everything looks good - even liver and beets), and obsession to eat before doing anything else.

Cravings

By definition, a craving is an intense and prolonged desire or appetite. The soul also has cravings. The lonely soul craves friends, companionship, acceptance, validation, attention and affirmation. Cravings compel behavior until satisfied. In other words, cravings don't go away until something fulfills them. The challenge with cravings of the heart is knowing how to satisfy them. When the body craves protein, eating meat satisfies; but satisfying the cravings of the soul is much more complex. Isaiah 55 reminds us of this complexity that is actually quite simple:

> Come, all you who are thirsty, come to the waters;
> and you who have no money, come, buy and eat!
> Come, buy wine and milk without money and
> without cost. Why spend money on what is not
> bread, and your labor on what does not satisfy?
> Listen, listen to me, and eat what is good, and
> your soul will delight in the richest of fare. Give

ear and come to me; hear me, that your soul may
live. (Isa. 55:1-3a)

The context is clearly that of spiritual feeding, "that your soul may live." Also, the prophet declares that food which satisfies the soul is free. This free nourishment for the soul is found in God and his word, "come to me, hear me." The complexity comes in recognizing things other than God in which we seek nourishment for the soul: "why spend money on what is not bread and your labor on what does not satisfy?" (Isa 55:2).

Loneliness, for example, cannot be satisfied in a lasting way through any human relationship because friends move away, divorce happens and people die. Even people with many friends and good marriages feel lonely and crave lasting, authentic intimacy. Humans are relational creatures by God's design, so we will always crave relationship; but human relationships do not satisfy and, since the fall in Eden, seem to create frustration as much as peace. The difficulty is that we expect others to satisfy our relational cravings and when they don't, we resort to manipulation and control to satisfy our relational hunger. Seeking to satisfy loneliness in a relationship with anyone other than God will ultimately lead to disappointment.

Loving wives not only recognize their husbands' need for affirmation, respect and validation but seek to impart those things to their husbands. But the most loving wife is still broken by sin herself and will fail to affirm, respect and validate her husband every time he needs it. Loving husbands recognize their wives' cravings for attention, tenderness, love and protection. But even the most sensitive husband will fail to be attentive, tender, loving and faithfully protective at all times because he, too, is broken by sin. Relational cravings are fully satisfied only in Christ.

The human craving for significant purpose and identity can only be fully satisfied in Christ. That's why Paul said, "For through the law I died to the law so that I might live for God. I have been crucified with Christ and I no longer live, but Christ lives in me" (Gal. 2:19-20a). Living for the glory of God is the purpose for which humanity was created (Isa. 43:7). Living for any other purpose leaves the soul craving. Paul died to himself, his former identification and purpose so he might be identified in Christ and live for Christ's purposes.

John speaks about the cravings of the world for things:

> Do not love the world or anything in the world. If anyone loves the world, the love of the Father is not in him. For everything in the world - the cravings of sinful man, the lust of his eyes and the boasting of what he has and does - comes not from the Father but from the world. The world and its desires pass away, but the man who does the will of God lives forever. (1 John 2:15-17)

Materialism does not satisfy, but, as John D. Rockefeller expressed when asked how much was enough, "Just a little bit more!" Humans never have enough until we discover satisfaction in God and then, "You will be like a well-watered garden, like a spring whose waters never fail. The Lord will guide you always; he will satisfy your needs in a sun-scorched land and will strengthen your frame" (Isa. 58:11). Unsatisfied cravings can lead to anger and grumbling. Anger is a response to unmet expectations. Grumbling is a way we express our disappointments. When you recognize anger and grumbling in your life, it's time to feed on Jesus. Pour out your anger and grumbling to Jesus. Tell him why you are disappointed. Then petition his Spirit to satisfy you.

Learn to recognize cravings of the soul and allow those cravings to compel you to feed on Jesus. Cravings require satisfaction, and lasting satisfaction is only found in Christ. Turn from pursuing satisfaction in anything but Jesus by pouring out to him how you have sought fulfillment in others, yourself or things. Empty your soul and then petition Jesus as Moses did in Psalm 90:14, "Satisfy us in the morning with your unfailing love, that we may sing for joy and be glad all our days."

Emptiness

A hungry person feels empty. Emptiness is another symptom of a need to feed. Cravings of body or soul seem more particular and are usually a desire for a specific something, but emptiness is more general, a less pronounced awareness of the need for nutrition. When I feel empty in my soul, I know I need

169

something, I'm just not sure what. Filling the emptiness becomes trial and error, one experimental taste after another, and that is what makes it spiritually dangerous.

The empty soul that feels bored might pursue more activity. When more activity fails to nourish, the person may try even more activity. Busyness is often an unrecognized attempt to fill an empty soul, but more activity requires more energy, which causes more hunger. Activity is usually counterproductive for the hungry soul. Instead of nourishing, moving from one activity to another at a frenzied pace just creates more hunger for something that truly satisfies. Doing doesn't satisfy; feeding does. The "unsatisfied doer" often feels he can never do enough to please a spouse, employer, parents, people or God. Doing doesn't honor God, receiving from him does.

Long term emptiness may compel a person to constantly pursue "new starts." New starts include everything from redecorating a room or getting a new hair style to changing jobs or moving to a new community. Empty people live with a continual, low-grade discontentedness. Changing circumstances may satisfy in the short term, but over time the nagging emptiness resurfaces, compelling even more change. Some folks seem to need continual change. All change comes with a certain sense of loss, which can result in despair and an acute dissatisfaction with everything. The more acute the feeling of emptiness, the more drastic change the person pursues. Taken to an extreme, these drastic attempts to fill the soul lead to immoral activity and even crime.

Fear may be another symptom of emptiness and the behavioral opposite of busyness. Anxiety can be difficult to detect within the soul, but all forms of fear are restrictive. People who struggle with fear do not possess the internal fortitude to initiate relationships or even conversations. They wrestle with feelings of inferiority. Phrases that float through their minds include: "I don't have anything to contribute, no one wants to hear what I think, my opinion doesn't matter." Fears keeps people grounded from soaring on to new heights in Christ. Such persons are prisoners to stagnancy because they are too afraid to risk proclamation or other relational overflows of the life of Christ. They are spiritual hoarders, too afraid to share, step out or take relational risks. They are content with some measure of the life of Christ but are too afraid to risk more to gain more. Anxiety that leads to self-protection keeps them hidden from people and God, restricting the fullness of what God wants to pour into them. Such lovers of status quo will never fully experience the exhilarating courage that comes from the life of Christ, because they will never fully step out into the realm of the unknown.

A more religious, but equally ineffective, attempt to fill the emptiness of the soul can be the pursuit of knowledge, biblical knowledge. Knowledge in itself does not nourish the soul, not even Bible knowledge. The Bible reveals the source of life, and that life is Christ. Words of Christ illuminated to the heart by the Spirit of Christ do nourish, but knowledge apart from the life of Christ does little to feed and nourish spiritual vitality. Knowledge makes us better informed. The life of Christ, expressed through illuminated truth, feeds our souls.

Other symptoms of spiritual emptiness include apathy and greater temptation. Avoiding church, Bible reading, prayer, and other believers because "I don't feel like it" is symptomatic of spiritual emptiness. Looking for "a fix" in something else is giving in to temptation. "I don't care" and "that looks good" are symptoms that it's time for a Jesus meal.

Learn to recognize how you seek to fill the emptiness of your soul. Assess your activity. Ask yourself why you are doing what you do. Auger deep within your own soul to discover activities that are motivated by a desire for fullness. Pour out those unwise motivations and petition the Spirit to fill you. Flee from pursuing those things and consume Christ instead.

Lethargy

Longer periods without eating create lethargy. The body doesn't have as much energy because it hasn't been properly fueled. Spiritual lethargy grips many. Scripture tells us in Romans 12:11 to never lack zeal but to keep our spiritual fervor serving the Lord. One of the more obvious signs of widespread spiritual lethargy is a lack of committed service to Christ, his Church and his mission - a lack of overflow. Where the Spirit is, the Spirit flows. Where there is no consuming Christ there is no life of the Spirit (John 6:53). The source of spiritual lethargy is our lack of consuming Christ. Don't expect spiritual vitality, fervor and zeal without spiritual nutrition.

A blessed, elderly husband and wife in our congregation serve in multiple areas: instrumental music, choir, meal preparation, greeting, office assistance, visitation, funerals, encouragement cards, unlocking all facility doors early Sunday mornings and more. The wife even plays piano for another smaller congregation in town. I've never heard this couple say, "It's time for someone else to do it!" They do not lack zeal but continue to serve the Lord with spiritual fervor just as they have for decades. An eighty-four-year-old man in our congregation imparts enthusiasm for life in Christ every time he steps into the building, and his zeal is contagious to everyone. Say his name and the people of our congregation will instantly smile. His daily feeding routine includes reading and pondering five Psalms and a chapter of Proverbs each morning. Then he reads a chapter from a gospel and an epistle each afternoon.

I still have one grandparent living, my Grandmother Boyers, who just turned 103. Recently, Grandma was coaching me on how to present the gospel at her funeral (if I'm still alive when she dies, and I'm beginning to wonder). She said, "People need to know it's not just about going to Church but knowing Jesus. Matthew, (she's one of two people on the planet allowed to address me as Matthew), I want you to get to the 'nitty gritty' of people knowing Jesus. I talk to Jesus all day long. I know Jesus more and more the older I get." Recently, Grandma heard of a single woman in the community who needed some food for her family, so Grandma prepared a week's worth of homemade meals and had them delivered to the needy person (Grandma still drives but doesn't have the strength to carry a week's worth of food.) This amazing woman still has zeal to serve the Lord because the life of Christ has been forming in her for over a century.

Did you know Moses was eighty years old when God called him to lead the people out of Egypt? Daniel was over eighty when he received fresh vision from God, and John was an old man when he wrote the book of Revelation. These great people continued to serve Christ with zeal in their old age because they spent a lifetime consuming Christ. If your zeal to serve Christ is lacking, it's time to enhance your spiritual diet. Don't quit or leave it up to someone else. Don't take more time for yourself or demand that others serve you. Your lethargy is communicating your need for nourishment. Feed on Jesus.

Weakness

The Apostle Peter addressed another important symptom of spiritual malnutrition: weakness in fighting temptation. 2 Peter 1:3-4 says, "His divine power has given us everything we need for life and godliness . . . so that through them [his own glory and goodness] you may participate in the divine nature and escape the corruption in the world caused by evil desires." We participate in his divine nature by feeding on that nature. Only then can we escape corruption that comes through falling prey to evil desires. It is the divine nature of Christ forming within us that brings victory over temptation. When Jesus was tempted, he responded to the Devil with the word of God saying, "Man does not live on bread alone, but on every word that comes from the mouth of God" (Matt. 4:4). Jesus knew the "nutritional power" of God's word was the strength of resistance to temptation. Sometimes guilt and shame cripple us with weakness. Unconfessed sin or failure to appropriate Christ's forgiveness can make us more vulnerable to temptation. We think, "What's the use. I already failed. I'm already guilty." Such thoughts usually compel more sinful behavior, not less. A feeding on the forgiveness of Christ is the only lasting remedy to guilt or shame.

Fatigue

A more pronounced symptom of spiritual malnutrition is fatigue. Without food, even after twenty-four hours, the body goes into conservation mode by slowing down consumption of vital energy. Fatigue is the feeling of the body conserving energy. Spiritual fatigue slows believers down in fulfillment of mission. When we grow tired spiritually we rest by "taking ourselves out of the game" for awhile. It's spiritually saying, "I just can't do it right now. I need a break." When a person is too exhausted to function physically we often say, "Sit up and eat something" because we know food creates energy. Feeling spiritual fatigue? Sit up and eat.

Some common ways spiritual fatigue presents itself are through discouragement, feeling overwhelmed, anxiety, worry, frustration and burnout. Few things sap internal strength like discouragement. Discouragement seems to be a key weapon of our enemy. Paul was concerned about discouragement coming on believers in Ephesus: "I ask you, therefore, not to be discouraged because of my sufferings for you, which are your glory" (Eph. 3:13). Apparently, Paul was concerned that the suffering he experienced in bringing the gospel to them might discourage the believers, most likely through fear or even guilt that Paul had to suffer for them. The next few verses in Chapter 3 of Paul's letter to them are a prayer in response to this potential discouragement. Notice the focus of the prayer below is for the life of Christ to dwell in them that they might know the vast measure of Christ's love for them and be filled with the fullness of God:

> For this reason, [potential of discouragement] I kneel before the Father . . . I pray that out of his glorious riches he may strengthen you with power through his Spirit in your inner being, so that Christ may dwell in your hearts through faith. And I pray you, being rooted and established in love, may have power, together with all the saints, to grasp how wide and long and high and deep is the love of Christ, and to know this love that surpasses knowledge - that you may be filled to the measure of all the fullness of God. (Eph. 3:14-19).

Paul understood the antidote to discouragement is fullness of the life of Christ forming and shaping itself within the believer. The life of Christ forming in the human heart enables the soul to persevere, even when circumstances are discouraging.

We are more vulnerable to frustration when we are tired. Let frustration compel you to rest in Jesus. He doesn't need you to do more for him, just to rest in and be nourished by him. Too much outflow without enough inflow will always lead to fatigue. Eat more.

Pain

Paul, James and Peter remind believers about the opportunity to rejoice in suffering (Rom. 5:3, Jas. 1:2, 1 Pet. 4:13). Rejoicing in suffering is not some "pie in the sky" wish, but hope, a confident expectation we should have in Christ. The New Testament writers not only taught us to rejoice in suffering but modeled it for us. They considered it a glory to suffer for Christ (Eph. 3:13, 1 Pet. 4:12-14). E. M. Bounds reminded us that "Trouble is God's servant . . ." (Bounds 18). God uses trouble to work good in our lives. Trouble and suffering are tools God uses to form the life of Christ in us (Jas. 1:3-4, Rom.5:3-5, 1 Pet. 1:6-7).

Physical pain is often due to dehydration, since a healthy body is 60% fluid, but dehydration can be hard to recognize. Fever usually accompanies physical dehydration. Fever hinders the body from functioning effectively. Despair is the fever of the soul. A despairing person tries to function but the despair keeps him from being effective. When despair and the pain that causes it are not poured out on Christ, depression can set in. Depression is dark, hopeless, debilitating and so very painful. Pondering the gospel can redeem pain, pouring out the soul expresses pain and praise redirects the soul from pain. But just as with physical dehydration, the best solution is fluid, lots of it. Petition the Holy Spirit. Have elders and godly consumers of Christ intercede for you. You need a fresh outpouring of living water to flush your soul.

Another common source of spiritual pain is feeling overwhelmed by life, problems, activity and pressure. 2 Corinthians contains an amazing list of things that overwhelmed Paul. Reading 2 Corinthians 11:23-12:8 reveals sources of what overwhelmed Paul: harder than normal work, frequent imprisonment, severe flogging, multiple near death experiences, two hundred lashes from Jewish resistance, beatings with rods, stonings, being shipwrecked, a night and day in the open sea, constantly on the move, danger from nature, bandits, countrymen and false brothers, sleeplessness, hunger, thirst, cold, nakedness, pressure of concern for churches he'd planted and, perhaps the worst, a persistent "thorn in the flesh" for which he prayed three times to be removed. God did not remove that thorn from Paul but used it to strengthen Paul with the life and power of Christ. The Lord did reveal to Paul the purpose of the thorn, "to keep me from becoming conceited" (2 Corinthians 12:7a). Through consistent petitioning, Paul was given a new perspective on all that overwhelmed him.

Remember, trouble is God's servant. Once we apprehend and embrace that truth and the personal power of the one who spoke that truth, we can rejoice in suffering and endure incredible trials that would overwhelm anyone. Jesus' answer to Paul's three-time petition was, "'My grace is sufficient for you, for my power is made perfect in weakness'" (2 Cor. 12:9a). Paul then said, "Therefore I will boast all the more gladly about my weaknesses, so that Christ's power may rest on me. That is why, for Christ's sake, I delight in weaknesses, in insults, in hardships, in persecutions, in difficulties. For when I am weak, then I am strong" (2 Cor. 12:9b-10). The key to enduring overwhelming busyness, trouble and pressure that overwhelm and cause pain is the life and power of Christ within us, life that is formed as we consume Christ. Ask Jesus for relief from the things that overwhelm and thank him if he provides relief; but be assured if Jesus doesn't supply relief, he will perfect his strength in your soul, forming you more into his likeness through your pain.

Everything Looks Good

Another symptom of dehydration is the mirage factor. Severe dehydration and heat create illusions of water that a thirsty person may chase. When a person is really thirsty, everything and anything looks satisfying to him! This can be very dangerous in the spiritual realm because desperately thirsty souls resort to extremes to find satisfaction. Don't trust the mirages of the world. Money, sex, and power are mirages; they do not satisfy.

"Everything looks good" thirst causes people to live on the moral edge of lasciviousness. Western culture has embraced this smorgasbord approach to satisfying the soul. The mindset of western culture that compels people to think, "I deserve to be happy" is embraced as a justifiable entitlement when in reality it is a confession of a hungry soul. "Buy, take or get what you want in pursuit of your own happiness" seems more appropriate for our coins than "In God we trust."

176

This "everything looks good" pursuit of satisfaction is rationalized within the church under the guise of God blessing his people materially, but material blessings or sex or power cannot feed the soul. We westerners have become compulsive about the pursuit of happiness. We'll try anything and everything to make us happy. The mirage of "everything looks good" leads to an even more dangerous starvation of the soul that is all consuming.

Desperation

Proverbs 29:18 says, "Where there is no revelation, the people cast off restraint." Spiritually dehydrated people throw off restraint because they are not drinking the Spirit. Where there is no consuming the revelation of God, (word and Spirit), there will be no restraint. It is amazing what hunger and thirst will drive people to do. Most divorces and substance abuse issues are hungry and thirsty people searching for satisfaction. Men and women will do vile, immoral and illegal things to quench the parched soul. Rational people will go to irrational lengths to find satisfaction. Nothing else matters to them. Malnutrition and dehydration drive the soul like nothing else because the pursuit becomes about survival.

The best way to avoid the dangers of extreme neediness that drives immoral obsession is to consistently feed on Jesus. Learn to consume Christ steadily to avoid acute hunger that compels unrestrained, obsessive choices. Well-fed people are never tempted to eat tree bark (or beets, for that matter). Well-nourished husbands and wives don't go looking for immoral relationships. Busy, stressed people who pour out their hearts to Christ and receive the filling of his Spirit have no need of stress relief from alcohol or other substances. People who feed on Jesus, like Paul, do not look for immoral or illegal satisfaction even when they experience ridiculous amounts of trouble but, rather, delight in the power of Christ at work within them.

Not all driven people are compelled by blatantly immoral or illegal behavior. Some are driven by the pursuit of power at home, in the workplace or even in "friendly" sports competition. For those driven by power, every relational interaction is about gaining the upper hand. Failure is intolerable for such people and can have a devastating effect on them. They tend to overexert. They are "workaholics." They are obsessed. Eventually overexertion causes them to hit a wall and they collapse. Too often, the overachiever just steps out of the game to find relief. Escapism can devastate his family and work. What's needed is refocus and rejuvenation. Gatorade was created to replenish vital electrolytes during a break from activity to get the person "back in the game." Our Gatorade (Holy Spirit) renews our perspective and rejuvenates the soul to get us "back in the game."

When your soul feels malnourished and dehydrated, feed on Jesus. Learn to identify the symptoms. Pour out all the spiritual junk food you have consumed in an effort to feed your soul and petition in the Spirit of Christ. When everything starts to look good to your soul instead of sampling from the worldly smorgasbord available to you, turn to Christ and embrace his life forming within you.

Dysfunction that Necessitates Special Feeding

Like the body, the soul can malfunction. Most people push through the annoyance of minor infections like a head or chest cold without much interruption in routine. Energy levels are lower because the body is using energy to fight the infection, but most endure the annoyance of a runny nose, congestion and cough by careful eating and the assistance of medication.

Spiritual infections can be thought of as things external to us that affect our soul in the short term. Annoying people who come across our path or drivers who get in our way, lack of attention from a spouse or harsh words from a work associate are minor unmet expectations like colds. We push through the annoyance, recognizing it as short term. When something breaks, like a car or appliance, we are annoyed; but once the thing is fixed, it frees our soul. Pour out such frustrations to the Lord Jesus as they come along.

A portion of my daily feeding on Jesus includes pouring out such frustrations and annoyances. It's important to recognize these and entrust them to the Lord (Ps. 62:8) in order to move past them quickly. When annoyances and frustrations are allowed to remain in the heart, evil may gain a foothold (Eph. 4:26-27). It's also important to keep feeding on Jesus in response to frustration and annoyance. Most mothers press children to eat and drink lots of fluids when fighting a cold. Push through "spiritual colds" by pouring out and feeding on Jesus with extra intentionality.

Viruses

A flu virus is a different matter. Influenza takes people out of their routine for awhile. The flu requires fluids and bed rest. The flu puts us on our backs with fever, pain, weakness and other nasty symptoms. We feel miserable and cannot function normally. We know we'll get better in a week or so, but we also realize we'll be miserable until then. There's not a lot that can be done to accelerate healing from influenza; it has to be endured. The best thing is rest and wise dietary choices while the body reacts to and fights off the virus.

Spiritual viruses also take us out of our routine. Conflict, stress and criticism act like viruses of the soul that require a dramatic change until the symptoms dissipate. When the body is infected with the flu, it screams, "Rest!" When the soul is infected, it screams, "Rest!" Spiritual rest is not taking time off from Jesus, but going to him with greater intentionality and zeal. "Come to me, all you who are weary and burdened, and I will give you rest" (Matt. 11:28). When spiritual influenza strikes you, don't turn from Jesus because of anger, frustration or disappointment; rather, press deeper into him. Pour out the "virus," feed wisely, with intentionality, and drink plenty of fluids, the living water of the Holy Spirit. Petition the comfort, healing, forgiveness and love of Jesus to fill your soul. Don't just keep going with your normal routine because spiritual influenza can lead to more serious things. Plan a half day of prayer. Turn off the television and read through the entire book of Revelation in one sitting. Take a prayerful walk. Spend your lunchtime praying instead of eating.

Injury

Bodies get injured; so do souls. Injury usually involves acute pain and results in some type of bodily malfunction. Ignoring an injury only exacerbates it. If unattended, injuries can result in

179

infection, disability, inactivity or even death. Injuries require initial treatment and some form of rehabilitation.

Spiritual injuries happen when we least expect, just like physical injuries. Things that injure the soul include rejection, criticism, failure, grief, relational breakdown and other types of trauma. Injuries to the soul create pain and anxiety as we wonder how we will heal. Will I be OK? How will I function? How long will it take until I'm better? What is the best rehabilitation strategy? Should I be doing something else to treat this?

People notice physical injuries and ask, "What happened?" Usually, the injured person doesn't mind telling the story (especially men, who love to tell their broken bone, concussion and suture stories). It is good to tell the story of soul injuries. People find healing in recounting the circumstance of the deceased's passing. Those going through divorce long to talk about it with someone. The criticized or slandered want someone else to know their pain. Verbal pouring out to others often includes blame, questioning or even retaliatory slander and vilification. Injury compels verbalization, but all too often people seek healing through verbal vengeance. Hurting people hurt people.

Tell your story of pain and trauma to Jesus. He cares deeply for you and understands your pain. He will heal your soul as you pour out your heart to him. Jesus always listened to people tell their stories before healing them. Hearing their stories didn't benefit the omniscient Jesus but the people who told the stories. Pouring out the story of your soul injury to Jesus promotes healing because Jesus has the power to heal your soul. Other people do not.

People who were healed by Jesus sought him out. Some went to great lengths, like the four friends who lowered the paralytic from a hole in the roof. Those who didn't have the faith to go or respond to Jesus were not healed. Jesus is the ultimate healer, so go to him. Tell Jesus your story and ask him for healing. Ask and it will be given you, seek and you will find. Healing takes time, and Jesus' healing may not occur on our time frame. Trust him to heal in his way and time.

Wounded people need unconditional love from the supportive community of Jesus Christ. If you've been wounded, find a trusted brother or sister in Christ who loves you deeply and tell them your story. Ask that person to help you find healing in Jesus. Share spiritual meals in Christ with that person who loves you. If a wounded sibling in Christ comes to you, invite him to pour out his heart to Jesus with you. Take initiative and invite him to consume Christ with you for a few months. We know how to encourage others by inviting them to the dinner table with us; how much greater to invite them to the table of the Lord with us.

Spiritual injury requires significant rehabilitation. Cooperate fully with Jesus in rehabilitation. Spiritual rehabilitation includes forgiveness (Matt. 18:21-22), reconciliation initiated by the injured party (Matt. 18:15) and avoidance of bitterness (Heb. 12:15). Forgiveness, reconciliation and avoiding bitterness are not easy but are necessary rehabilitation. Many people want healing but are unwilling to cooperate with Jesus in rehabilitation. After healing, Jesus usually gave some instructions of "rehabilitation" to the one healed (go show yourself to the priest, go and sin no more, stop sinning or something worse may happen to you). These activities are difficult, like any effective rehabilitation routine. It takes great internal strength to rehab effectively. Strength for rehab of the heart comes from the fullness of the Spirit and his illumination of the word to our hearts. When the Spirit impresses on the soul the need for forgiveness, reconciliation and avoidance of bitterness, he also gives the strength to accomplish these rehab activities.

Petition Jesus' healing and the power of the Spirit to rehabilitate. Believe his word of rehab and obey it. The Bible is our rehabilitation manual. Rehab is hard and takes a lot of energy. Respond with courage and initiative to the relational instruction of Jesus, who will "push" you through rehabilitation. Don't give up, even when it gets hard; keep working the therapy Jesus gives you - the commands of scripture. A popular cliché in the world of rehabilitation is, "No pain, no gain." Let Jesus have his way with your injury. Learn from it. Find healing in him. Trust him and his timing.

Internal malfunction

Malfunctioning organs, joints, muscles and bones within the body usually require intervention, such as corrective surgery or a long term program of medication, to restore proper function. Body parts that have been damaged, weakened or diseased can sometimes be repaired (heart bypass surgery), other times restored through medication and sometimes replaced through transplant.

A heart surgeon told a man in our congregation who needed bypass surgery that it was impossible because of the prior heart damage. The surgeon told him the damaged heart tissue had hardened and trying to suture a new artery to that area would be like trying to suture a rubber garden hose to a concrete sidewalk. Such vivid imagery illustrates how the human body can be damaged and how limited medical resources are to fix certain malfunctions. Due to his age and overall health, a transplant was not an option, so the patient was told he had to live with the damaged heart.

We don't have to live with a damaged spiritual heart, because there is no problem which our savior cannot intervene to fix, restore, heal or even replace. Consider a badly damaged heart, hardened by sin, unable to function as designed. Is there any cure, any intervention for the human heart? The prophet Ezekiel answered the question definitively with words from God, "I will give you a new heart and put a new spirit in you; I will remove from you your heart of stone and give you a heart of flesh. And I will put my Spirit in you and move you to follow my decrees and be careful to keep my laws" (Ezek. 36:26-27). The Lord Jesus is able to perform radical, life-saving transplants of the heart. Transplant of the heart is the only way to restore human function to the original design God intended.

A couple in our congregation divorced because of hardness of heart. Through the pain of divorce, the husband learned to soften his heart and consume Christ. He kept on loving his ex-wife and praying for her. He knew her heart was hard, so he began praying Ezekiel 36:26-27 personally for her by quoting the words of the text with her name inserted. After he had prayed this scripture multiple times daily for two years, her heart changed. They began dating again. Months later the wife shared the circumstances by which her heart changed.

She was at home, mopping her kitchen floor on her hands and knees. She prayed while she worked, pouring out her heart to the Lord. She began crying out for the Lord when it happened: "It felt like God cracked open my chest, put his hands on my cold, hard heart and melted it. From that moment on everything changed." This was a direct and miraculous answer to the husband's Ezekiel 36 prayer. That new heart warmed for her former husband. I had the privilege of officiating their remarriage ceremony about a year later. The Lord Jesus can fix broken hearts, soften hard ones and replace dead ones.

Many things harden spiritually malfunctioning hearts: physical, verbal or sexual abuse, unbelief and cynicism, unresolved pain and bitterness, pride, unrecognized narcissism, betrayal, unresolved conflict, stubbornness and rebellion. Physical, emotional or psychological illness can harden the heart. At some point, the hardness becomes almost irreversible, making the only solution a transplant - and that is the hope of the gospel. Too often we think of the gospel as influencing the heart, softening the heart, opening the heart or altering the heart, but the gospel ultimately removes the broken, hardened, dead human heart and replaces it with a soft heart of flesh, responsive to and compelled by the Spirit, who forms the life of Christ in the new heart.

The Christian life begins with a heart transplant performed by the regenerative Spirit of the Almighty God. Follow-up is vital after any major heart surgery. Consuming Christ is how believers nurture, feed and strengthen the new heart given them by God. Only a new heart can help a person who has been hardened and wounded by abuse, cynicism and unresolved pain or bitterness. Follow-up treatment within the body of Christ, the Church, will be necessary following the transplant. Deeply hardened people need biblical instruction, discipleship, love and long term care to live gospel-centered lives free from the pain of their past. Consuming Christ with good friends who enjoy spiritual meals together becomes particularly significant for those who were hardened by wickedness against them.

Infectious Disease

Many diseases are mostly incurable. Medication and therapy help, but the patient must learn to live with the disease. Sin will eventually be eradicated when Jesus returns but, until then, we are called to fight against it. Every human being has been infected by the disease of sin.

Two members of my immediate family fight against multiple sclerosis. MS presents in waves or outbreaks from time to time. Both family members inject themselves with a drug three times per week that minimizes symptoms of the disease for a period of time. Consuming Christ has that same effect on the soul. As the life of Christ grows to prominence within the soul and overcomes the sin nature, the life of Christ holds back and is dominant over sin. This process concludes only when the believer is glorified with Christ; but by feeding on Jesus, progress is accelerated and the disease of sin nearly masked. The consumer of Christ has real spiritual power over sin.

A few years ago, my body fought against an unknown African infection after I had spent some time in the primitive bush of West Africa. For about three months I ran a low-grade fever and struggled with severe swelling in my wrists and feet. I had scheduled a snow skiing day with my two youngest teenagers and was concerned that I'd have to cancel because my feet would not fit into my ski boots. The day before we skied, I started on a steroid treatment prescribed by my doctor. After just three doses, the swelling and pain in my ankles disappeared completely and the next day I skied circles around my athletic children. They were ready to call it a day by 4:00 p.m., but I wanted to ski more because I felt so good. I still had the infectious disease, but the steroid so masked it that I didn't care, nor did it hinder my enjoyment. That's what the gospel does for us spiritually. We still have the disease of sin until we are glorified in Christ; but, as we consume Christ, sin is overpowered by the ever-forming, predominant life of Christ within us so that our joy and function are unhindered.

About a week after my steroid regimen ended, the fever and swelling in my feet returned. Of course, I called my doctor, who graciously prescribed another round of steroids. After three cycles, the mysterious African fever subsided and I've

184

experienced no symptoms since. But the disease of sin never goes away. It is within us, in others and all around us, so we must continue to consume Christ and live dependent on him who is forming within. My family members with MS have adjusted their diets and lifestyles in order to manage the disease. They live normal, functional lives by wisely ingesting medication and the food they need.

Disabilities

Some people are born with physical disabilities; all are born with spiritual disabilities. Those who struggle with disabilities need special help. Because we are disabled by sin, we need help in all areas of life. As fallen creatures, we do not have within us what it takes to be faithful and loving spouses, faithful and productive workers, godly parents or loving neighbors and friends. Fallen humans tend to forget or minimize their own depravity. Authentic Christian relationships are different because believers recognize everyone's disabilities of sin. All are in need of redemption, all are sinful, there is no one righteous (Rom. 3:23). Therefore, there is no reason for pride, arrogance or comparison. Sin renders us all the same, in need of redemption and regeneration. The feeding believer knows that Jesus died not only for his sin, but also for the sins of those who sin against him. Grudges, resentment or withheld forgiveness have no place in the church. We have all sinned and are saved only by the grace and love of our savior. Instead of resenting, believers are free to help others with our sin disability through love, forgiveness and reconciliation.

Help is a prominent word in scripture, especially in the psalms. David and the other psalmists often petitioned for help, help the Lord gave. Many psalms express thanks and praise to God for his direct intervention and help. There are numerous Old Testament stories of God helping through external intervention. God often changed circumstances as a way to help in the Old Testament. Today, many believers long for that same kind of help that changes circumstances. I can testify of God's providential changing of circumstances around me and I'm very grateful for those times, but far more frequent in my experience are the times when God has helped me by changing ME. Oswald

Chambers said in *My Utmost for His Highest*, "It is not so true that prayer changes things as that prayer changes me and I change things" (August 28). God most often helps me by changing me, which is a far greater thing than circumstantial manipulation.

God helps me with my spiritual disabilities by changing my attitude and perspective more than the circumstances around me. Philippians 4:7 promises peace that transcends all understanding when I pour out my anxiety to my Lord. If we read Philippians 4:6 out of context, "Do not be anxious about anything, but in everything, by prayer and petition, with thanksgiving, present your requests to God," we might wish the next verse would say, "And God will change your circumstances to give you peace." But the promise is greater than circumstantial change, it is internal peace. Internal peace trumps the anxiety of any and all situations. That's a much greater gift than external change.

Paul encouraged Timothy to guard the word of truth that had been planted in him by saying, "Guard it with the help of the Holy Spirit who lives in you" (2 Tim. 1:14b). The internal fullness of the Holy Spirit is a continual source of help to the feeding believer. Internal help is better than external. With internal empowerment and peace from the Holy Spirit, the feeding believer can rise above the stress of circumstances. I still embrace God's external help and am grateful for it when he dispenses it; but with or without providential manipulation of external circumstances, God always gives peace when I pour out my anxiety over my disabilities to him. He is our helper externally and internally as the life of Christ and the power of the Spirit form within us.

Doctors, dieticians and physical fitness experts teach us to eat right because what and how we eat is vital to physical health. Exercise, medication or treatment are ineffective without intentional feeding according to a proper diet and schedule. Learn to recognize the symptoms of spiritual malnutrition, dehydration, injury, malfunction and disease, then respond by feeding on Jesus. Over time, failure to feed from the right source exacerbates spiritual hunger and compels the consumption of more "junk food for the soul." Learn to recognize the symptoms of spiritual hunger within your heart, turn from junk food, (repentance), and feed your soul with Christ.

"Drink plenty of fluids" is good advice for the sick body and the sick soul. Psalm 81:10 says, "I am the Lord your God, who brought you up out of Egypt. Open wide your mouth and I will fill it." Jesus Christ, broken and poured out, is the solution to spiritual malnutrition and dehydration of the soul. God longs to pour the life of Christ into your soul, but he won't force-feed or nourish you intravenously. You must open your mouth and consume. So open wide!

QUESTIONS FOR THOUGHT AND INTERACTION
Chapter 9

1. In what ways are you most vulnerable to spiritual dehydration?

2. What can you do to manage cravings of your soul for anything but Jesus?

3. How can you recognize emptiness in your soul? How about lethargy?

4. What fatigues your soul? What can you do about that?

5. What mirages do you chase trying to satisfy your soul?

6. What ongoing dysfunction or disease of your soul (memories, scars, pain, resentment) do you need most to combat by consuming Christ?

Conclusion

"Take and eat; this is my body"
(Matthew 26:26)

Nothing lives without feeding and drinking - it is fundamental to all creation. This truth is illustrated throughout creation from microscopic organisms to massive mammals. Scientists look for extraterrestrial evidence of water because we know that without water, nothing lives. Living creatures feed in a variety of ways. Methods vary greatly from species to species, but the necessity of eating and drinking remains constant.

The necessity of consuming Christ is, therefore, consistent with all creation. God is about life and God has offered humans new life in Christ. But as with every other living creation of God, spiritual life requires eating and drinking. Living things appropriate life from God through feeding and drinking, so it is not surprising to realize that in John 6 Jesus used the idea of belief synonymously with feeding so that we can say with confidence feeding is believing.

We've seen how the Old Testament expressed this fundamental truth by pointing ahead to Jesus as Passover Lamb, manna from heaven and the rock from which water flows; but, remember, the Passover lamb was to be eaten in totality. Manna had to be gathered daily to be consumed. Water from the rock had to be swallowed to impart life in desert places. Scripture records how God's people repeatedly turned from him as the fountain of life (Ps. 36:9) to seek life in other sources, what Jeremiah described as broken cisterns that cannot hold water (Jer. 2:13). Throughout history people have fed on the wrong things. Whether idols, help from other nations or more prominent empty wells of today's culture such as money, sex and power, humans seek life from things that do not nourish.

Passover and other Old Testament feasts were commanded to be annual reminders of God as the only source and fountain of life and nourishment. The feasts were celebrations of the sufficiency of God to impart life and reminders to the people to feed on and trust God instead of other people, idols or by digging their own wells. The feasts of Unleavened Bread, Passover,

Firstfruits and Tabernacles all pointed to Christ as eternal life from God. Jesus connected the Feast of Tabernacles to himself in John 7:37-39: "On the last and greatest day of the Feast, [Tabernacles] Jesus stood and said in a loud voice, 'If anyone is thirsty, let him come to me and drink. Whoever believes in me, as the Scripture has said, streams of living water will flow from within him.' By this he meant the Spirit, whom those who believed in him were later to receive." Notice that Jesus used the word "believe" in the present continuous tense, synonymous with coming to him and drinking.

Professing Christians often seek protection from the "Passover blood" of Jesus without any commitment to feed on the Passover lamb. We still dwell in desert places without acknowledging God as the source of life in the midst of the desert. Christian culture has redefined belief to mean something less than the continual response of feeding on Christ that Jesus intended and taught in John 6 and throughout the gospels. We confess Christ by acknowledging facts about him, but fail to believe by feeding on him. Western Christian culture seeks blessings of God without faithfully drinking from God as the fountain of life.

Through David's psalms and other poetic literature of the Old Testament, God teaches us to pour out our sinful obsessions of feeding on and drinking anything other than him. The prophets of the Old Testament remind us that our default setting is to dig our own wells, to seek help from others and to give ourselves to idols. They also point us to Jesus and him alone for life. It is the prophets who give us promises of hope such as Ezekiel 36:26, "I will give you a new heart and put a new spirit in you; I will remove from you your heart of stone and give you a heart of flesh. And I will put my Spirit in you and move you to follow my decrees and be careful to keep my laws." This promise of change from the inside out, wrought by the Spirit of God, was fully revealed in the New Testament gospel of Jesus Christ.

The gospels declare the story of the one to whom the Old Testaments points. That story culminates with Jesus being broken and poured out. The hours leading up to the crucifixion of Jesus included the last supper, where Jesus instructed his disciples to eat his body and drink his blood. Jesus used the metaphor of broken bread and poured-out wine in John 6:53-58 to instruct us to consume Christ. Following that instruction, Jesus proceeded directly to the garden, where he modeled pouring out the heart to God in times of awful anxiety and extreme stress. Jesus showed us through petition how the Father empowers with sufficient courage to carry out his will. Jesus was looking for any other way but, when assured by the Father there was no other, he moved forward with incredible courage of the Holy Spirit. Jesus taught and modeled for us how to feed on God as he fed on his Father. He moved forward to be broken and poured out that we might feed on him.

Paul and the other New Testament writers worked and wrote as they did so that Christ might be formed in us (Gal. 4:19). We've been instructed to work out our salvation in Philippians 2:12, and the continuation of the sentence in verse 13 describes how that will happen, "for it is God who works in you to will and to act according to his good purpose." It is God, the life of Christ working within the believer, who brings salvation to fullness within us. We cannot do what God does in our souls anymore than we can do for our bodies what food does for them. Our responsibility is to feed our bodies with healthy food and feed our souls with Christ, who will form himself within and transform us from the inside out. We are passive recipients of the life of Christ at work within us. The energy of Christian living ought not be dispensed on moralism, "trying harder," but on emptying ourselves before God (pouring out the heart) and petitioning the Holy Spirit of Christ to fill us and form the life of Christ within us.

A culminating metaphor appropriate to the theme of this book is the future wedding feast of the Lamb referenced by Jesus in the parable of the wedding banquet (Matt. 22:1-14, Luke 14:15-24) and as a literal feast in the future kingdom of God (Luke 13:29). The angel who revealed future realities to John also spoke of this banquet to come, "Blessed are those who are invited to the wedding supper of the Lamb!" (Rev. 19:9a). Feeding on Jesus now is preparation for that great banquet. The banquet will be the ultimate fellowship experience of Jesus and his bride, the Church. All true believers will be at the table and will enjoy the feast together - it will be the ultimate feeding experience with our

Lord and each other! The key to enjoying this blessed event is to make sure you don't miss it, and being there requires only one thing - responding to the personal invitation to feed on Jesus (John 6).

What I said in the introduction I will repeat here: Love for malnourished believers compelled me to write this book. Jesus taught that many would be invited to the heavenly banquet but only a few would be chosen. Outside the heavenly banquet room there will be weeping and gnashing of teeth (Luke 13:24-30). Those who thought they'd be first in may be last or won't get in at all. The way in is narrow and only a few find it. That's not because the way is difficult, but rather because it is so foreign to our sinful nature which defaults to earning our way. Response to the invitation of grace is faith—ongoing, dependent trust in the work and person of Christ. I've become convinced that such faith means feeding on Jesus - believing is feeding. We've no other hope of being properly clothed for the banquet except for the life of Christ formed within us, and that happens as we feed on him.

Until that glorious future day, we should allow our spiritual hunger and cravings to drive us to Christ and feed on him. Proverbs 16:26 says, "The appetite of laborers works for them; their hunger drives them on." Allow your emotional, spiritual and physical appetites to drive you to Christ, for only in Christ will you be satisfied. Learn to recognize your spiritual thirst and go to the fountain of living water. When the heat of desert times comes, go to the well. Drink of the Spirit as you feed on Christ. He will make you like a well-watered garden (Isa. 58:11), like a tree planted by water (Jer. 17:8, Ps. 1:3), like a fruitful branch (John 15:5) and like a fruitful tree (Matt. 12:33). Revelation 22:1-2 teaches that wherever the Spirit of living water flows there is life and fruit: "Then the angel showed me the river of the water of life, as clear as crystal, flowing from the throne of God and of the Lamb down the middle of the great street of the city. On each side of the river stood the tree of life, bearing twelve crops of fruit, yielding its fruit every month. And the leaves of the tree are for the healing of the nations."

Abundant life in this world is only possible in the Spirit dispensed through Christ's work on the cross and poured into thirsty believers who swallow it down. There is no life to be found in this world; all is desert and drought. One of the most vivid illustrations of this I've witnessed in thirty years of ministry was in the life of Randy. I met Randy in the basement of his home when he was in marital crisis. My wife was upstairs consoling Randy's wife, LeAnn, who had just learned from Randy that he'd been having a long distance affair. Randy was quite open with me about the affair. He confessed that he still loved LeAnn but found in the affair something exciting and passionate that he'd never known before.

That was the first of many meetings with Randy, most in a quiet corner of the local McDonald's early in the morning. There Randy told me more specific details of the affair than I ever wanted to know. He seemed to be captured, apprehended by it. It wasn't really love for the other woman, just impassioned excitement that seemed to hold him prisoner. He knew it was wrong and displeasing to God, but he couldn't stop. Randy loved his wife and children and he knew this affair would ruin his family, but still he couldn't let go. He wanted to end the affair and often tried, but the forbidden passion that was poisoning his life and soul continued to lure and hold him in a death grip. After months of guilt, shame, separation, "schizophrenic-like" behavior and the condemnation of death, God revealed himself to Randy in a very special way on a golf course in Florida. The following is the account of the experience in Randy's own words:

> The affair had ended, temporarily, and I was longing for peace in my life. I was searching. I had been meeting with a great friend who constantly put God's word in front of me. A common theme in several of the verses was "water." One passage that stood out was Isaiah 58:11 – "The Lord will guide you always; he will satisfy your needs in a sun-scorched land and will strengthen your frame. You will be like a well-watered garden, like a spring whose waters never fail." Oh, was I ever dry and sun-scorched! When was my soul going to be watered? I needed to hear from God and was finally ready to listen.

A couple of free afternoons gave me time to think and do something I really enjoy – golf. Florida was experiencing a severe drought, even by their standards. It had been over thirty days of summer heat without rain. The golf pro and I discussed the drought and he told me the forecast called for a slight chance of rain, (only about ten percent). When I asked him if I was going to get wet he just laughed and said it "would be nice, but not a chance."

I made the turn to the 10th hole and noticed the sky turning a little gray. On the tee box at hole #15 I felt a sprinkle. The sprinkle turned into a drizzle and then a downpour. Other golfers, making their way back to the clubhouse through the downpour, gave me the "this guy is crazy" look while I stood on the 15th tee and soaked it in. I couldn't tell if the moisture on my face was more from the rain or from my tears – I was being watered! Florida needed the rain, and my soul needed it more. God was speaking to me and I was being filled!

I finished the round drenched but did not care a bit. I'd never experienced a more intimate "God moment" than I had on the golf course that day. I suddenly felt like the "well-watered garden" spoken of in Isaiah. I wish I could say that everything went well after that experience. It didn't, but my wife and I eventually reunited are now celebrating twenty-two years of marriage. Rain is not the same to me anymore. In fact, rain on the golf course brings a smile to my face and, at times, tears of joy, reminding me of Christ's presence in my life.

Randy's story reminds me of Ezekiel 47, where the prophet describes the river of living water that flows from the very presence of God, illustrated by the Temple. I believe this river is the same river John described in Revelation 22, issuing from the throne of God alongside which grew twelve crops of life giving fruit. When the river Ezekiel saw emptied into the Dead Sea, the water there became fresh. The Dead Sea cannot support life. It's a dead body of water, hence its name. But when the river of living water flowed into it, everything changed. Ezekiel said, "Swarms of living creatures will live wherever the river flows. There will be large numbers of fish, because this water flows there and makes the salt water fresh; so where the river flows everything will live" (Ezek. 47:9).

My friend Randy was living in a desert of death polluted by sinful minerals of immorality and unrestrained passion; but when Randy poured out his heart and began to petition in the Spirit of Christ, everything changed. Where there had been death, life started to form. Today, Randy is a faithful father, godly husband, faithful community servant, leader in his church and personal friend, whose very presence reminds me of the transforming power of Jesus when we consume Christ and drink his Spirit. Where the river flows, everything lives!

QUESTIONS FOR THOUGHT AND INTERACTION
Conclusion

1. How does the future wedding feast of Jesus compel you to consume Christ now?

2. How has this book challenged your faith as an ongoing response to the Fountain of Life God?

3. What will you do in response to this book to continuously feed on Jesus?

4. How is experiencing the life of Christ forming in you? How is his life changing you and those around you?

Appendix A
Topical list of David's Psalms Helpful for Pondering and Pouring Out

Chapter	Description	Verse
Psalm 3	Safety in Christ	3:3
Psalm 4	Sleep in peace	4:8
Psalm 5	Security in Christ, not people	5:3
Psalm 6	Internal exhaustion	6:2
Psalm 7	Salvation from an enemy	7:9
Psalm 8	Known by the Great Creator	8:1
Psalm 9	Justice against wicked enemies	9:10
Psalm 11	Refuge in Christ instead of fear	11:1
Psalm 12	Loneliness of righteous living	12:8
Psalm 13	Emotional turmoil turned to peace	13:6
Psalm 14	Lord's perspective on people	14:2
Psalm 15	Righteous living	15:1
Psalm 16	My all in all in Christ	16:2
Psalm 17	Vindication in Christ	17:2
Psalm 18	Equipped by the Lord, my rock	18:2
Psalm 19	Lord revealed in creation and word	19:1
Psalm 20	The Lord's responsiveness	20:7
Psalm 21	Rejoicing in the Lord	21:1
Psalm 22	Suffering of Christ	22:11
Psalm 23	Good Shepherd	23:1
Psalm 24	The Lord's ownership of all	24:1
Psalm 25	Hope in the Lord	25:3
Psalm 26	Examine Me	26:2
Psalm 27	Confidence in Christ	27:1
Psalm 28	Trust in the Lord	28:7
Psalm 29	Worship the Lord	29:2
Psalm 30	Reasons to sing to the Lord	30:4
Psalm 31	Rescue me as I commit to you	31:2
Psalm 32	Confession of sin	32:5
Psalm 34	Protection when afraid	34:7
Psalm 35	The Lord my Defender	37:4
Psalm 36	Refreshment in the Lord	36:4
Psalm 37	Delight in the Lord	37:4
Psalm 38	Weightiness of Guilt	38:4

Appendix A
Topical list of David's Psalms Helpful for Pondering and Pouring Out

Chapter	Description	Verse
Psalm 39	Stewarding time, talent, treasure	39:6
Psalm 40	Waiting on the Lord	40:1
Psalm 41	Help in sickness	41:3
Psalm 51	Brokenness	51:17
Psalm 52	Prosperity when betrayed	52:8
Psalm 53	Foolishness without the Lord	53:1
Psalm 54	Triumph in trouble	54:7
Psalm 55	Casting cares on God	55:22
Psalm 56	Trusting when afraid	56:3-4
Psalm 57	Encouragement in despair	57:8
Psalm 58	Righteousness is worth it	58:11
Psalm 59	Deliverance from the enemy	59:1
Psalm 60	Victory in battle	60:12
Psalm 61	Listen to me, Lord	61:1
Psalm 62	Pour out to the Lord	62:8
Psalm 63	Thirsty for God	63:1
Psalm 64	Complain to God	64:1
Psalm 65	Provider God	65:9
Psalm 68	Empowerment from God	68:35
Psalm 69	I'm sinking, drowning, worn out	69:1-3
Psalm 70	I'm needy	70:5
Psalm 86	Compassionate and gracious God	86:15
Psalm 101	I will sing	101:1
Psalm 103	Benefits of the Lord	103:1-2
Psalm 108	Steadfast before the Lord	108:1
Psalm 109	Heal my wounds	109:22
Psalm 110	My personal Lord	110:1
Psalm 122	Go to worship	122:1
Psalm 124	Helper God	124:8
Psalm 131	Quiet before the Lord	131:2
Psalm 133	United in the Lord	133:1
Psalm 138	My purpose in the Lord	133:8
Psalm 139	Search my heart	139:23

Appendix A
Topical list of David's Psalms Helpful for Pondering and Pouring Out

Chapter	Description	Verse
Psalm 140	Justice from the Lord	140:12
Psalm 141	Undivided heart for the Lord	141:4
Psalm 142	Cry out to the Lord	142:1-2
Psalm 143	Teach me Lord	143:10
Psalm 144	Equipped by the Lord	144:1-2
Psalm 145	Praise the Lord	145:3

Appendix B
Pleasant Feelings
List of Feeling Words for Pouring Out

OPEN	HAPPY	ALIVE	GOOD
understanding	great	playful	calm
confident	gay	courageous	peaceful
reliable	joyous	energetic	at ease
easy	lucky	liberated	comfortable
amazed	fortunate	optimistic	pleased
free	delighted	provocative	encouraged
sympathetic	overjoyed	impulsive	clever
interested	gleeful	free	surprised
satisfied	thankful	frisky	content
receptive	important	animated	quiet
accepting	festive	spirited	certain
kind	ecstatic	thrilled	relaxed
	satisfied	wonderful	serene
	glad	flattered	
	cheerful	bright	
	sunny	blessed	
	merry	reassured	
	elated		
	jubilant		

LOVE	INTERESTED	POSITIVE	STRONG
loving	concerned	eager	impulsive
considerate	affected	keen	free
affectionate	fascinated	earnest	sure
sensitive	intrigued	intent	certain
tender	absorbed	anxious	rebellious
devoted	inquisitive	inspired	unique
attracted	nosy	determined	dynamic
passionate	snoopy	excited	tenacious
admiration	engrossed	enthusiastic	hardy
warm	curious	bold	secure
touched		brave	
treasured		daring	
close		challenged	

Difficult / Unpleasant Feelings
List of Feeling Words for Pouring Out

ANGER	DEPRESSED	CONFUSED	HELPLESS
irritated	lousy	upset	incapable
enraged	disappointed	doubtful	alone
hostile	discouraged	uncertain	paralyzed
insulting	ashamed	indecisive	Fatigued
sore	powerless	perplexed	useless
annoyed	diminished	embarrassed	inferior
upset	guilty	hesitant	vulnerable
hateful	dissatisfied	shy	empty
unpleasant	miserable	stupefied	forced
offensive	detestable	disillusioned	hesitant
bitter	repugnant	unbelieving	despair
aggressive	despicable	skeptical	frustrated
resentful	disgusting	distrustful	distressed
inflamed	abominable	misgiving	woeful
provoked	terrible	lost	pathetic
indignant	in despair	unsure	tragic
infuriated	sulky	uneasy	in a stew
cross	bad	pessimistic	dominated
disrespected	sense of loss	tense	insignificant
boiling			unimportant

INDIFFERENT	AFRAID	HURT	SAD
insensitive	fearful	crushed	tearful
dull	terrified	tormented	sorrowful
nonchalant	suspicious	deprived	pained
neutral	anxious	pained	grief
reserved	alarmed	tortured	anguish
weary	panic	dejected	desolate
preoccupied	scared	injured	pessimistic
cold	worried	offended	unhappy
disinterested	frightened	afflicted	lonely
lifeless	timid	aching	grieved
	shaky	victimized	mournful
	restless	heartbroken	dismayed
	doubtful	agonized	

Works Cited

Billheimer, Paul. *Destined for the Throne.* Grand Rapids: Bethany House Publishers, 1996. Print.

Blackaby, Henry T. and Claude V. King. *Experiencing God.* Nashville: Lifeway Press, 1990. Print.

Bounds, E.M. *The Essentials of Prayer.* Radford: Wilder Publications, 2008. Print.

Calvin, John. *The Gospel According to St. John: 1-10.* Grand Rapids: William B. Eerdmans Publishing Co., 1995. Print.

Chambers, Oswald. *My Utmost for His Highest.* New York: Dodd, Mead & Company, 1963. Print.

Colson, Charles. *Against the Night.* Ann Arbor: Servant Publications, 1989. Print.

"Gospel-Driven Life, The." *Tabletalk.* February 2013: 70. Print.

Hillsong United. "Desert Song." *This Is Our God.* Hillsong, 2008. CD.

Jacoby, Matthew. *Deeper Places.* Grand Rapids: Baker Books, 2013. Print.

Keathley III, J. Hampton. *ABCs of Christian Growth.* Biblical Studies Press, LLC., 2002. Web. 30 July 2013.

Lane, Timothy S. and Paul David Tripp. *How People Change.* Greensboro: New Growth Press, 2006. Print.

Lewis, C.S. *Mere Christianity.* New York: HarperCollins Publishers, 1952. Print.

- - -. *Reflections on the Psalms.* New York: Harvest Books, 1986. Print.

Lewis, Gordon R. and Bruce A. Demarest. *Integrative Theology, Volume III.* Grand Rapids: Zondervan, 1994. Print.

Lovelace, Richard F. *Dynamics of Spiritual Life: An Evangelical Theology of Renewal.* Downers Grove: InterVarsity Press, 1979. Print.

Luther, Martin. *Day by Day We Magnify You: Daily Readings for the Entire Year: Selected from the Writings of Martin Luther.* Minneapolis, Augsburg Books, 2008. Print.

Marshall, Colin and Tony Payne. *The Trellis and the Vine.* Kingsford: Matthias Media, 2009. Print.

Murray, Andrew. *Experiencing the Holy Spirit.* New Kensington: Whitaker House, 1984. Print.